Led Zeppelin In Their Own Words

Compiled by Paul Kendall
& Dave Lewis

Exclusive Distributors:
Book Sales Limited
8/9 Frith Street,
London W1V 5TZ, UK.

Music Sales Corporation
257 Park Avenue South,
New York, NY 10010, USA.

Music Sales Pty Limited
120 Rothschild Avenue, Rosebery,
NSW 2018, Australia.

To the Music Trade only:
Music Sales Limited
8/9 Frith Street,
London W1V 5TZ, UK.

OMNIBUS PRESS
LONDON / NEW YORK / SYDNEY

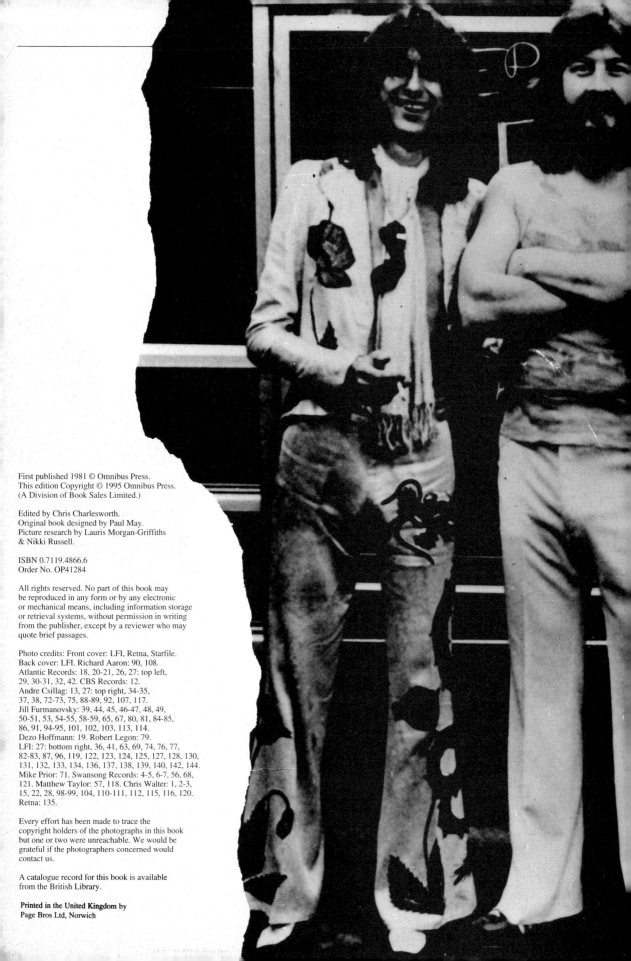

First published 1981 © Omnibus Press.
This edition Copyright © 1995 Omnibus Press.
(A Division of Book Sales Limited.)

Edited by Chris Charlesworth.
Original book designed by Paul May.
Picture research by Lauris Morgan-Griffiths
& Nikki Russell.

ISBN 0.7119.4866.6
Order No. OP41284

Photo credits: Front cover: LFI, Retna, Starfile.
Back cover: LFI. Richard Aaron: 90, 108.
Atlantic Records: 18, 20-21, 26, 27: top left,
29, 30-31, 32, 42. CBS Records: 12.
Andre Csillag: 13, 27: top right, 34-35,
37, 38, 72-73, 75, 88-89, 92, 107, 117.
Jill Furmanovsky: 39, 44, 45, 46-47, 48, 49,
50-51, 53, 54-55, 58-59, 65, 67, 80, 81, 84-85,
86, 91, 94-95, 101, 102, 103, 113, 114.
Dezo Hoffmann: 19. Robert Legon: 79.
LFI: 27: bottom right, 36, 41, 63, 69, 74, 76, 77,
82-83, 87, 96, 119, 122, 123, 124, 125, 127, 128, 130,
131, 132, 133, 134, 136, 137, 138, 139, 140, 142, 144.
Mike Prior: 71. Swansong Records: 4-5, 6-7, 56, 68,
121. Matthew Taylor: 57, 118. Chris Walter: 1, 2-3,
15, 22, 28, 98-99, 104, 110-111, 112, 115, 116, 120.
Retna: 135.

Every effort has been made to trace the
copyright holders of the photographs in this book
but one or two were unreachable. We would be
grateful if the photographers concerned would
contact us.

A catalogue record for this book is available
from the British Library.

Printed in the United Kingdom by
Page Bros Ltd, Norwich

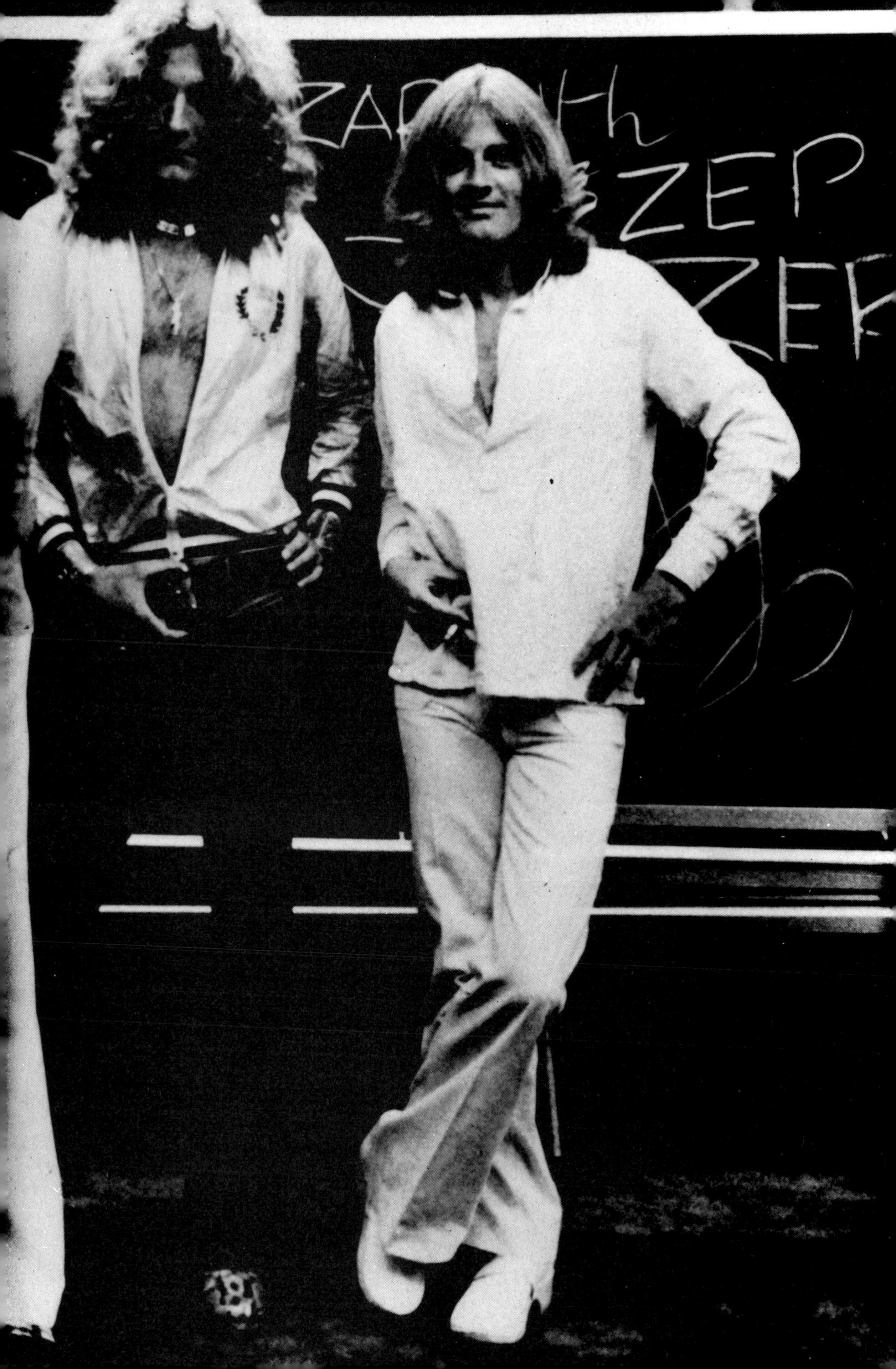
ZEP

Led Zeppelin were never great givers of interviews. In fact, for long periods during their twelve years together, they were as communicative as a silent Order.

John Bonham was rarely tempted away from his livestock and cars to speak to the media. John Paul Jones always made Greta Garbo seem like a relentless publicity-seeker. And the group's main spokesmen, Page and Plant, soon developed the knack of giving interviews without giving anything away.

Not for them the full-frontal candidness of The Who. The scathing wit of a Zappa. The flair for the sudden insight

or 'mot juste' of a Dylan or a Jagger.

If you're looking for an exposé on high jinks behind locked hotel doors, the lowdown on dabblings in magic and mysticism, the full truth about their private lives, controversy, rumour or hot gossip, you'll scour this volume in vain.

If any interviewer ever managed to extract such details from Led Zeppelin, the results were not committed to print.

What you will find, however, is the story of one of rock's legends, from the diverse beginnings to the tragic conclusion, told by the people who knew it best. *Paul Kendall*

Early Days

Jimmy Page: Somebody laid a very old Spanish guitar on us. I probably couldn't play it now if I tried. It was sitting around our living room for weeks and weeks. I wasn't interested. Then I heard a couple of records that really turned me on, the main one being Elvis's 'Baby Let's Play House' and I wanted to play it. I wanted to know what it was all about. This other guy at school showed me a few chords and I just went on from there.

I've read about many records which are supposed to have turned me on to play rock'n'roll, but it was 'Baby Let's Play House' by Presley . . . I heard that record and I wanted to be part of it . . . I knew something was going on. I heard that acoustic guitar, slap bass and electric guitar – three instruments and a voice – and they generated so much energy I had to be part of it. That's when I started.

Probably my greatest influence on acoustic guitar was Bert Jansch who was a real dream weaver. He was incredibly original when he first appeared, and I wish now that he'd gone back to things like 'Jack Orion'

once again. His first album had a great effect on me.

When I was at school I had my guitar confiscated every day. They would hand it back to me each afternoon at four o'clock. But I always thought the good thing about

guitar was that they didn't teach it in school. Teaching myself to play was the first and most important part of my education.

The nearest I ever came to an ordinary job was an interview I had, while still at school, for a laboratory assistant. But I chose The Crusaders instead until my health started playing up—I caught glandular fever.

You'd come off stage at the clubs and the caretaker would shout out 'Come on, don't hang about. If you're still here in ten minutes you'll be locked in for the night.'
     They had me doing things like arcing over backwards until my head touched the stage—all those silly things that groups used to do. We were driving around the country, sleeping in the van and all that sort of stuff. We had breakdowns on the M1 motorway . . . and that was great for a while, but eventually it knocks you out. I didn't have a good resistance to sickness and I came down with glandular fever. I just collapsed from exhaustion and fatigue. After only a few months with the band, I started to wonder if I could carry on much longer.

I was doing a lot of painting and drawing in what free time I had, and so I thought I'd go to art college, because a number of my friends had gone to art college anyway, and I thought . . . maybe this is it, maybe this is

my vocation. So I went—but of course I couldn't stop tinkering around with my guitar and I was still playing at the Marquee in a sort of interval band.
     I was involved in the old Richmond and Eel Pie Island sets—well, I used to play at those jazz clubs where The Kinks played and I'd always been in groups round the Kingston area. Kingston and Richmond were the two key places, really, but by that time I was well into the Marquee. It was a good scene then, because everyone had this same upbringing and had been locked away with their records, and there was something really new to offer. It just exploded from there.

I really wanted to be a fine-art painter. I was really sincere about that. I didn't tell anyone at the college that I played guitar or else they would have had me playing in the lunch hour. But gradually a conflict between music and art arose. When I first started art college the music scene was pretty depressing. Nobody was interested in Chuck Berry or Bo Diddley. All people

R&B revival restored my faith in pop music.

wanted was Top Twenty stuff and trad jazz. Then about a year later everything started to happen. The Stones broke through and there were the Liverpool and R&B scenes coming together. I enjoyed playing and the

One night somebody came along and asked me if I'd like to play guitar on a record. To tell you the truth, I can't even remember who it was. It was a nothing song, I remember that, and it became a minor hit. That led to other session offers and suddenly there were more than I could cope with—often as many as four or five a week.

If there were three sessions requiring guitarists going on at any time, Big Jim (Sullivan) would play one and the other producers would end up with . . . well, we won't mention any names. Without Big Jim they were desperate. When I came on to the scene, work quickly escalated. I became a new name. Big Jim had been carrying the whole weight on his shoulders and he was the only other young face on the scene.

I had work flooding in as they didn't have any young guys playing guitar. There was only one other young guitarist, and he was about twenty-six and had lost a lot of enthusiasm for playing. So I had all these groups asking me to play on their records, and I just took it and thought I might as well, because I can be a painter and starve the rest of my life, but I can always go back to it.

I didn't really do that much on Kinks records. I know I managed to get a couple of riffs on their album, but I can't really remember. I know that Ray didn't really approve of my presence. The Kinks just didn't want me around when they were recording. It was Shel Talmy's idea. One aspect of being in the studio while potential hits were being made was the press—too many writers were making a big fuss about the use of session men. Obviously I wasn't saying anything in the press, but it just leaked out . . . and that sort of thing often led to considerable bad feeling.

I was still getting the situation where a violinist session fixer, who really didn't know many other session musicians, would hear that there was a new guitar player around, and he'd book me for what turned out to be a ludicrous session—like muzak for supermarkets, or something like that. Things in that vein were just a headache and I shouldn't have been doing them.

    · The work was stifling. It was often like being a computer when you had no involvement with the artist. It should be stimulating to do sessions with other groups, but it wasn't working out that way.

Another problem was that for a while guitarists were becoming out of vogue at sessions. People had this obsession with something new, using sax sections and things like that. I rarely had the chance to roar into something. The sax players and violinists looked on me as some kind of joke with my feedback ideas.

I played a lot of rhythm guitar, which was very dull and left me no time to practise. Most of the musicians I know think I did the right thing in joining The Yardbirds.

Robert Plant: At thirteen and a half I liked girls all of a sudden and it all came down to attracting them the best way I could. So I grew my hair. It flopped down over my ears and was immediately chopped off by demand. I forgot about lessons for the next few years and kept joining pop groups.

There was this fellow called Terry Foster who came from not very far away from Kidderminster, my home village. Terry was an incredible eight-string guitarist. Instead of playing in the normal way, he used to play like Big Joe Williams with the instrument half on his lap. He was a horrible bloke at times, but he was a real white bluesman, and when I was fifteen I fell immediately under his spell. I suppose he was the one who really introduced me to this music.

My Dad used to drop me off at the Seven Stars Blues Club in Stourbridge and we used to wail away on 'Got My Mojo Working' and stuff like that. Chris Wood used to play with us, and Stan Webb and Andy Sylvester were in a competing band.

The Seven Stars Blues Club was really my initiation. Our group was called The Delta Blues Band. When we weren't doing that number, a guitarist and myself would go around all the local folk clubs playing 'Corinna Corinna', plus all those vulgar blues tunes like Petti Wheatstraw's stuff. When you look deeper into that kind of music you find it has a lot of the feelings which exist in blues. Then of course you realise that the blues field is a very wide one.

I was supposed to start training as a chartered accountant. Although I was young, really, I suddenly decided where I was going. I packed up the accountancy training after only a couple of weeks and I went back to college to get some more 'O' levels. It was getting to the stage where I only dared to go home at night because my hair was so long. So at sixteen I left home and I started my real education musically . . . moving from group to group, furthering my knowledge of the blues and other music which had weight and was worth listening to.

I'd been singing with a lot of groups and I'd written a few songs myself that didn't really have the right amount of balls behind them that they should have had. It really just went around the circles until I formed the first Band of Joy.

Living near Birmingham I got in with a lot of Jamaicans and I started to like the old Blue Beat. And we'd been doing a Darrell Banks number, something by Otis Clay and even Little Milton things. Of course, it was received everywhere with open arms. As a band we were all still learning – the drummer would slow the beat every now and then, and the guitarist played a few odd chords. He never really ever played 'Sunny' with the same chords on any two successive nights . . . God bless him.

The manager just told me I couldn't sing and sacked me from the group. I asked him to give me another chance but he wouldn't.

. . . The new band (Band of Joy Mk.II) decided to have painted faces on stage – before the arrival of The Crazy World of Arthur Brown. It went all right for a while, but we were frightening our audiences to death. This big fat bass player would come running on and dive straight off the stage. I was howling with laughter at the sight of him in kaftan and bell bottoms, billowing in the audience. The whole thing was absurd. I was driving the van as well and doing all sorts of jobs. We got in a fantastic guitarist, a good bass player, and Bonzo Bonham came in on drums.

For a long time there were duff promoters trying to keep them (Midlands groups) down, only booking them to play Kinks numbers and chart stuff all night. The Band of Joy managed to get about two gigs a week. It was only through Maureen, my wife, working that we kept going, or I'd have ended up a Belsen case.

Eventually we were getting between 60 and 75 quid a night. But it didn't keep improving. In the end I just had to give it up. I thought 'Bollocks! Nobody at all wants to know about us!' Bonzo went to work with Tim Rose.

Actually, I believed that I would be on the dole. But I wasn't going to give up. For a while I was living off Maureen, God bless her. Then I did some road making to earn some bread. I actually laid half the asphalt on West Bromwich High Street. All it did for me was give me 6/2d per hour, an emergency tax code and big biceps. All the navvies would call me the pop singer. It was really funny.

My own influences were more blues people like Snooks Eglin, Robert Johnson, Tommy McClellan and even Bukka White. Bukka had a really nasal thing. His records from the 30s like 'Fixing To Die' and 'Bukka's Jitterbug' have a nasal vocal approach which I sometimes use.

I got hold of a Buffalo Springfield album. It was great because it was the kind of music you could leap around to, or you could sit down and just dig it. I thought to myself 'This is what an audience wants and this is what I want to listen to'. Then I got the first Moby Grape album, which was a knockout . . . the guitar playing and everything was very good. It fitted together so well. It was the spirit of it that I reacted to, I think. I had loved old blues, but all of a sudden I couldn't listen to old blues any more. It really was a big change . . . now I was sobbing to Arthur Lee and Love doing 'Forever Changes'.

John Bonham: I've wanted to be a drummer since I was about five years old. I used to play on a bath salt container with wires on the bottom, and on a round coffee tin with a loose wire fixed to it to give a snare drum effect. Plus there were always my Mum's pots and pans. When I was ten, my Mum bought me a snare drum.

My Dad bought me my first full drum kit when I was fifteen and a half. It was almost prehistoric, most of it was rust. Now I really do look after my drums, and people who don't, annoy me. As soon as I left school I decided I was going to be a drummer and I was very determined. In Terry Webb and The Spiders we used to wear purple jackets with velvet lapels. The singer wore a gold lamé jacket, and we all had greased hair and string ties.

When I left school I went into the trade with my Dad. He had a building business and I used to like it. But drumming was the only thing I was any good at, and I stuck at that for three or four years. If things got bad I could always go back to building.

I had a group with Nicky James, an incredible lead singer. But we had so much of the equipment on hire purchase, we'd get stopped at night on the way back from a

gig and they'd take back all the PA.

Nicky had a big following then and he could sing any style. But he couldn't write his own material. We used to have so many clubs we could play around Birmingham in those days. Lots of ballrooms too. All those places have gone to the dogs – or bingo.

I was so keen to play when I left school, I'd have played for nothing. In fact I did for a long time, but my parents stuck by me.

I swore to Pat that I'd give up drumming when we got married, but every night I'd come home and just sit down at the drums. I'd be miserable if I didn't.

John Paul Jones: I've got to own up, the first record that really turned me on to bass guitar was 'You Can't Sit Down' by Phil Upchurch, which has an incredible bass solo and was a good record as well. It was very simple musically, but the record had an incredible amount of balls.

As a bass player I wasn't influenced by a lot of people because it was only in the mid to late sixties that you could even hear the bass on records. I had a number of obvious jazz influences – most of the good jazz bass players influenced me in one way or another . . . Charles Mingus, Ray Brown, Scott La Faro. I even got into jazz organ for a while until I couldn't stand the musicians any more and I had to get back to' rock'n'roll.

I discovered that musical arranging and general studio direction were much better than just sitting there and being told what to do. I'd been doing some sessions with Donovan. The first thing I really did with him was 'Sunshine Superman'. I happened to be on the session as a bass player and I ended up doing the arrangements. The arranger they'd picked for the session really didn't know about anything. I got the rhythm section together and we went from there.

Peter Grant: I had a bad, bad education . . . it was all mixed up with being evacuated during the war and my circumstances . . . I don't remember father, but I have a marvellous Mother who I've been able to look after really well now. When I was

thirteen I became a stage hand at the Empire Croydon theatre in London. I also tried working in a sheet metal factory, but after only five weeks I knew it just wasn't in me. Then I got a job at Reuters, taking photos round Fleet Street . . . I ran around to the customers with wet pictures hanging over my arms. I was also employed as a waiter.

Then came National Service in the RAOC. I became corporal in charge of the dining hall. I enjoyed my time there because it was a very cushy number. I worked a season at a holiday camp, which was dreadful. Then I stinted for a time as entertainment manager at a hotel in Jersey. Then back to London to work in a Soho coffee bar – Tommy Steele was discovered there. Mickie Most was a waiter and I was on the door . . . they paid us ten shillings and a meal a night. Being doorman at Murray's Cabaret Club was good fun too – I wasn't married then, and what with me being the only man around and about forty girls backstage, it was all right.

I was also a wrestler for about eighteen months when I needed some money, and then I got into acting. I doubled for Robert Morley in films and took on small parts in the TV series 'Dixon of Dock Green' and the Sid James/Tony Hancock series. I even played in the box office breaker 'The Guns of Navarone', but filming's not for me. Getting up at six a.m. and flogging it down to Pinewood Studio or somewhere – it's too much.

I was invited to be tour manager for several early American rock acts – Gene Vincent, Little Richard and Jerry Lee Lewis. After that I started managing, more by chance than anything else . . . I was finishing off working for an agent and I heard a group in Newcastle called The Alan Price R&B Combo, and eventually I managed them and later they became The Animals.

I just kinda came around to it. With all the odd jobs I'd done, it just gravitated that way. You don't just wake up in the morning having been a salesman or a dentist and say 'Hey, I'm going to manage groups'. You've got to move around the show business scene and that I think I've done.

The Yardbirds

Jimmy Page: I was offered the chance to join The Yardbirds when Eric (Clapton) left, but I turned it down because I didn't like the way the invitation was put to me. Their manager came over and said 'Oh, Eric's having a holiday'. 'Holiday' was the manager's clever little euphemism for the fact that Eric had split the group. If I hadn't known Eric, or hadn't liked him, I might have joined. As it was, I didn't want any part of it. I liked Eric quite a bit and I didn't want him to think I'd done something behind his back.

Eric came to my place when I lived in Epsom. We did some recordings between the two of us on a small Simon tape recorder with two channels, just home stuff. We did quite a few instrumentals with distortion and stuff. When the group

(Bluesbreakers) split and went to Decca, I'd already told Immediate that I'd been recording with Eric at my house. They said 'Well, don't forget those tapes belong to us, because Eric's still under contract to us'. So I had to give them the tapes, which had to have overdubs as several of the tracks were out-takes of the same number. They put a write-up, that I was supposed to have done, on the back and released it as part of a Blues Anthology. Eric and I got split writing on the tunes, but I don't remember getting any money out of it. I don't know if Eric did.

They (Yardbirds) were a good band to go and see. Then came this great night at an Oxford or Cambridge Union dance, I can't remember which, and Keith Relf was incredibly pissed. Everyone was dressed up

in dinner jackets and Keith was rolling around the stage, grappling with the mike, blowing his harmonica in all the wrong places and making up nonsense lyrics. He was shouting 'Fuck!' at the audience and eventually he just collapsed back into the drum kit.

It was great, just fantastically suitable for the occasion, I thought. But instead of everybody seeing the humour of it – as three members of the group and myself did – the bass player, Paul Samwell-Smith, just blew up and said 'I can't stand this any more. I'm going to leave the group and if I were you, Keith, I'd do the same thing'. Samwell-Smith was always after musical precision and adherence to a strictly rehearsed neatness, and it was more than he could take, it was the last straw. He'd just had enough and decided to quit.

After about two hours' rehearsal we played at the Marquee club, and once I started playing everything was all right.

The switch (from bass to lead) was necessitated earlier than planned. We were playing a gig at the Carousel Club in San

Francisco, and because Jeff (Beck) couldn't make it I took over lead that night and Chris Dreja played bass. It was really nerve-racking, because this was at the height of The Yardbirds' concert reputation and I wasn't exactly ready to roar off on lead guitar. But it went all right and after that we stayed that way. When Jeff recovered it was two lead guitars from then on.

One time in the dressing room I walked in and Beck had his guitar up over his head, about to bring it down on Keith Relf's head, but instead smashed it on the floor. Relf looked at him with total astonishment and Beck said 'Why did you make me do

that?'. Fucking hell. Everyone said
'Goodness gracious, what a funny chap'.
We went back to the hotel and Beck
showed me his tonsils, said he wasn't
feeling well and was going to see a doctor.
He left for LA where we were headed in
two days time anyway.

When we got there, though, we
realised that whatever doctor he was
claiming to see must have had his office in
the Whiskey. He was actually seeing his
girlfriend, Mary Hughes, and had just used
the doctor bit as an excuse to cut out on us.

The thing is, prior to my joining The
Yardbirds, apparently he had pissed
around on stage quite a lot – knocking over
his amps, just walking off and whatever. At
the time I came in, he was in a rut . . . I
think he felt a bit alien, in a way. I'm not
sure, but I think so. When I joined he
pulled himself together and was far more
disciplined, especially when I went on
guitar . . . he didn't want to go walking off
then. Instead he went to the other extreme
and started messing about offstage,
generally being late, not turning up until
the end of the session, et cetera.

These sort of things went on and it
must have revived all the previous
antagonism between him and the rest of the
band. I think that and a couple of other
things – especially the horrible wages we
were being paid – helped to bring about his
behaviour, which had obviously stewed
behind everybody's back.

I didn't even know about it, but by the
time we got to LA they had already decided
they didn't want to work with him any
more. They were just totally adamant and
there was nothing at this particular point
that either Beck or I could say to make the
rest of the group change their minds. Beck
wasn't saying anything anyway, because he
didn't have very much of an excuse.

We had a meeting and when it was
over Beck got up to leave and asked me if I
was coming too. I said 'No, I'm going to
stay behind', because I wanted to try to
work it out. Actually, it probably would
have been better if I had left, but at that
time I just really thought they could be
talked back into it if I told them the more
positive aspects of what happened and
what could be if we kept Jeff in the group.

Pete Grant: I started managing The Yardbirds in 1966. They were not getting hit singles, but they were already into the college scene here and the underground scene in America. Instead of trying to get plays on all that Top 40 rubbish, I realised there was another market. The Yardbirds were, in fact, the first British group booked into the Fillmore in San Francisco. Otherwise everybody just played hops.

Jimmy Page: Peter was working with Mickie Most and was offered the management when Most was offered the recording, of which the first session on our behalf was 'Little Games' and the first on Beck's behalf was 'Love Is Blue'. I'd known Peter from way back in the days of Immediate because our offices were next door to Mickie Most's, and Peter was working for him. The first thing we did with him was a tour of Australia and we found that suddenly there was some money being made after all this time.

In the studio I don't think we ever really had enough time to get together a good account of ourselves. We never rehearsed material for an album, it was like leaving Mickie Most to come up with the material. It's easy to be wise after the event, but when Donovan albums sounded so good, we figured we could probably trust Most to do as well for us. Maybe Donovan was just more headstrong in doing what he wanted. A lot of those things like 'Ha Ha Said The Clown' and 'Ten Little Indians' were done as experiments. He suggested that we try them and see what happens, but we just knew they wouldn't be any good.

If you've ever heard that album ('The Yardbirds With Jimmy Page Live At The Anderson Theater'), you'll know why we had it stopped. What happened was, Eric said to us 'Can we do a live LP?' and they sent down the head of their light music department to supervise it. We had an agreement that if the results were good, they could release the album . . . but if not, they'd just file it away.

Of course, it was terrible. This character who'd been recording stuff like 'Manuel's Music Of The Mountains' was strictly into muzak and the concert itself was bad. He'd done things like hanging one mike over the drums so none of the bass drum came through, and he'd miked up a monitor cabinet on my guitar instead of the proper amp through which I was playing all the fuzz and sustained notes . . . so all that was lost and we all knew it was just a joke. But this fellow assured us it would be all right. 'It's amazing what you can do electronically', he said.

Then we went to listen to the master tapes and there were all these bullfight cheers dubbed on it every time there was a solo and it was just awful. You'd play a solo and then this huge 'Raah' would come leaping out at you. There was one number where there was supposed to be utter silence in the audience and this guy dubbed in the clinking of glasses and a whole club atmosphere. But we had the right all along to say whether it would be released or not, and made them shelve it.

It just got to the point where Relf and McCarty couldn't take it any more. They wanted to go and do something totally different. When it came to the final split it was a question of begging them to keep it together, but they didn't. They just wanted to try something new. I told them we'd be able to change within the group format. Coming from a sessions background I was prepared to adjust to anything. I hated to break it up without even doing a proper first album.

I tried desperately to keep them together. The gigs were there, but Keith in particular would not take them very seriously, getting drunk and singing in the wrong places. It was a real shame. The group were almost ashamed of the very name, though I don't know why. They were a great band. I was never ashamed of playing in The Yardbirds.

There's still a lot of magic attached to The Yardbirds' name, and I find it amazing. I saw that group crumble—not in popularity—and I couldn't believe it when someone said to me that if The Yardbirds had stayed together a bit longer it could have been the biggest group ever. But I can see that it might possibly have happened—if we'd stayed together.

Forming Led Zeppelin

Jimmy Page: We were going to form a group called Led Zeppelin at the time of 'Beck's Bolero' sessions with the line-up from that session. It was going to be me and Beck on guitars, Moon on drums, maybe Nicky Hopkins on piano. The only one from the session who wasn't going to be in it was Jonesy, who had played bass. Instead

Moon suggested we bring in Entwistle as bassist and lead singer as well, but after some discussion we decided to use another singer. The first choice was Stevie Winwood, but it was decided he was too heavily committed to Traffic at the time and probably wouldn't be too interested. Next, we thought of Stevie Marriott. He was approached and seemed full of glee about it. A message came through from the business side of Marriott, though, which said 'How would you like to play guitar with broken fingers? You will be if you don't stay away from Stevie'. After that the idea just sort of fell apart. Instead of being more positive about it and looking for another singer, we just let it slip by. Then The Who began a tour, The Yardbirds began a tour, and that was it.

Peter Grant: I always had the most respect and admiration for Jimmy. I felt I was closer to Jimmy than any of the other members of The Yardbirds, and I had

immense faith in his talent and ability. I just wanted him to do whatever he felt was best for him at that time. Of course, it would have been a shame if he had decided to quit the business, but I don't believe the thought ever actually entered his head.

Jimmy Page: I was working at the sessions for Donovan's 'Hurdy Gurdy Man' and John Paul Jones was looking after the musical arrangements. During a break he asked me if I could use a bass player in the new group I was forming. Now John Paul is unquestionably an incredible arranger and musician—he didn't need me for a job. It was just that he felt the need to express himself and he thought we might be able to do it together. Sessions are great, but you can't get into your own thing. We talked about it and agreed that in order to give what we had to offer, we had to have a group. John simply wanted to be part of a group of musicians who could lay down some good things. He had a proper music training and he had quite brilliant ideas. I jumped at the chance of getting him.

John Paul Jones: I've rated Jimmy Page for years and years. We both came from South London, and even in 1962 I can remember people saying 'You've got to go and listen to Neil Christian and The Crusaders – they've got this unbelievable young guitarist'. I'd heard of Pagey before I'd heard of Clapton or Beck.

Jimmy Page: We (the Yardbirds) still had these dates we were supposed to fulfil. Around the time of the split, John Paul Jones called me up and said he was interested in getting something together. Also Chris (Dreja) was getting very into photography. He decided he wanted to open his own studio and by that time was no longer enamoured with the thought of going on the road.

I'd originally thought of getting Terry Reid in as lead singer/second guitarist, but he'd just signed with Mickie Most as a solo artist . . . quirk of fate. He suggested I get in touch with Robert Plant, who was then in a band called Hobbstweedle. When I auditioned him and heard him sing, I immediately thought there must be something wrong with him personality-wise or that he had to be impossible to work with, because I just couldn't understand why, after he told me he'd been singing for a few years already, he hadn't become a big name yet.

I went up to see Robert sing. They were playing at a teacher training college in Birmingham to an audience of about twelve people. It was a typical student set-up where drinking is the prime consideration and the group is only of secondary importance.

Anyway, I thought Robert was fantastic. Having heard him that night and having listened to a demo he'd given me of songs he'd recorded in his Band of Joy days, I realised that without a doubt his voice had an exceptional and very distinctive quality. So I asked him if he wanted to come down to Pangbourne and spend a few days talking things over.

The trouble was, I could play a lot of different styles but I really didn't know what to do. Sometimes I wanted to do a hard rock thing. At others, a Pentangle type thing. But as soon as I heard Robert Plant, I realised it was likely to be the former.

Robert Plant: We needed a drummer who was a good timekeeper and who really laid it down, and the only one I knew was the one I'd been playing with for years. Who was Bonzo Bonham. I got so enthusiastic that I hitched back to Oxford and chased after John, got him to one side at a gig and said 'Look, mate, you've got to join The Yardbirds'. But he wasn't easily convinced. He said 'Well, I'm all right here, aren't I?'. He'd never earned the sort of bread he was getting with Tim Rose before, so I had to try and persuade him. I had nothing to convince him with really, except a name that got lost in American pop history.

John Bonham: I had so much to consider. It wasn't a question of who had the best prospects, but which was going to be the right kind of stuff. Farlowe was fairly established and I knew Joe Cocker was going to make it. But I already knew from playing in Band of Joy with Robert what he liked, and I knew what Jimmy was into, and I decided I liked that sort of music better. And it paid off.

John Paul Jones: I wasn't into blues at first but soon followed Robert's interest in it. During our first rehearsals, any feeling of competition within the group vanished after one number.

Jimmy Page: We were sitting there kicking around group names and I suddenly remembered a name which Keith Moon had come up with some months earlier. We'd already considered Mad Dogs, but eventually came down to the fact that the name was not really as important as whether or not the music was going to be accepted. We could have called ourselves The Vegetables or The Potatoes. I was quite keen about Led Zeppelin . . . it seemed to fit the bill. It has something to do with the expression about a bad joke going over like a lead balloon. It's a variation on that. And there's a little of the Iron

Butterfly light-and-heavy connotation.

It was just a joke in England. We really had a bad time. They just wouldn't accept anything new. It had to be The New Yardbirds, not Led Zeppelin. We were given a chance in America. We started off at less than $1500 a night. We played for only $200 at one gig, but it was worth it. We didn't care. We just wanted to come over to America and play our music. I had assumed that even though the Yardbirds had been getting about $2500 a night, Led Zeppelin could only hope to start off at about the $1500 mark and work our way up from there.

Peter Grant: Before we got the LP, we couldn't get work here in Britain. It seemed to be a laugh to people that we were getting the group together and working the way we were. I don't want to name the people who put us down and thought we were wasting our time, but there were plenty of them.

I had a great belief in Jimmy Page both as a producer and a musician. John Paul Jones also had a great reputation. Robert had all the things together the very first time we took a look at him. John Bonham was ideal for the group.

I had been going to the States since 1964 when I went with The Animals. I learned a lot while I was there. By the time I got Zeppelin I knew America inside out. I knew Bill Graham, for example, and he has had a big influence on the business over there—not on rock itself, but on promotion. I knew if you got his two Fillmores, the Boston Tea Party and

Detroit, they were the most important places for the group.

Zeppelin started in the States on Boxing Day 1968. Three of the group had never been to America before and didn't know what to expect. They did a week with The Vanilla Fudge and the MCs did the usual stuff about a great new group from England, which didn't impress the people too much.

My instructions were to go over there and really blast them out. Make each performance something everybody remembered. They really did that. I have seen them at Boston do a four hour set and they would still have carried on playing but for exhaustion. Maybe they weren't the greatest thing ever on that first trip, but they got themselves across and the enthusiasm just exploded.

Jimmy Page: I can't really comment on just why we broke big in the States. I can only think that we were aware of dynamics at a time when everyone else was into that drawn-out West Coast style of playing.

I can tell you when I knew we'd broken through, though, which was at San Francisco. There were other gigs, like the Boston Tea Party and the Kinetic Circus in Chicago, which have unfortunately disappeared as venues, where the response was so incredible we knew we'd made our impression . . . but after the San Francisco gig it was just—bang!

We've been very lucky, it's been a very rapid success . . . it's amazing. Atlantic had a lot to do with it. They made sure people knew each member of the group as an individual. Also, I suppose there was added interest in myself being an ex-Yardbird, though at first in England this seemed to work against us, because the record-buying public seemed to lose interest as The Yardbirds kept having personnel changes and they sort of viewed us just as an extension of the early group. But for America it seems to have been a lucky combination, really.

We were a completely untried group of people who got together in the space of a few weeks to produce an album which really had only one ingredient that we were sure of—genuine enthusiasm. The secret of our success lies in the fact that we were unabashedly rock'n'roll and in our ability to interpret the excitement of those early rock sounds in the idiom of today.

John Bonham: I can't say how long it will last, but we'll go on for as long as we can. When I first joined the group, I didn't know Jimmy and I felt a bit shy. He was the big star and had been around for ages with the session thing and The Yardbirds. Now the group is closer than ever and there is a lot of scope for all of us.

John Paul Jones: If Jimmy had been incredibly insecure and really wanted to do a star number, he would have picked lesser musicians and just gone on the road and done the whole star trip. Once we'd realised that Jimmy's name was a boost to Led Zeppelin and became aware that we had a job to do, it worked out all right. I don't care if people don't recognise me or say 'Oh, you're not Jimmy Page'. I'm quite happy. I'd rather be in the background anyway. It's just my way. I've been into this too long to have ego trips.

Jimmy Page: Before they saw us in America there was a blast of publicity and they heard all about the money being advanced us by the record company. So the reaction was 'Ah, a capitalist group'. They realised we weren't when they saw us playing a three hour, non-stop show every night.

For anyone to imply that Led Zeppelin were pre-fabricated or hyped-up on a gullible public is grossly unfair. You can't compute or calculate for a situation like that or the chemistry which arises when you put together a band. The only people with a similar musical approach at the time were Cream, but I always felt their improvised passages used to go on and on. We tried to reflect more light and shade into the spontaneous pieces, and also a sense of the dramatic. If there was a key to why we made it, it was in that.

We could have been a bum group, No-one ever knows until you start working together. And if you're good, things start to happen.

The Albums

Led Zeppelin 1

Jimmy Page: The statement of our first few weeks together is our first album. We cut it in fifteen hours and between us wrote six of the nine tracks. It was easy because we had a repertoire of numbers all worked out and we just went into the studio and did it. I suppose it was the fact that we were confident and prepared to make things flow smoothly in the studio and—as it happened—we recorded the songs almost exactly as we'd been doing them live. Only 'Babe I'm Gonna Leave You' was altered, as far as I can remember.

It came together really quick. It was cut very shortly after the band was formed. Our only rehearsal was a two-week tour of Scandinavia that we did as The New Yardbirds. For material we obviously went right down to our blues roots. I still had plenty of Yardbirds riffs left over. On the first LP I was still heavily influenced by the earlier days. I think it tells a bit too. The album was made in three weeks. It was obvious that somebody had to take the lead, otherwise we'd have all sat around jamming and doing nothing for six months. But after that, on the second LP, you can hear the real group identity coming together.

All the things on the album are things that just seemed to be natural for the group to do. There's no reason to stick to one style of music nowadays.

Robert Plant: I don't think Jimmy was dominating anything as some have suspected. I was able to suggest things and the two of us re-arranged 'Babe I'm Gonna Leave You'. When we heard it back in the studio, we were shaking hands with our brains because it turned out to be so nice. It was really good to be able to get it off like that. It's been a good relationship all round. John Paul Jones has never worked with anybody like me before—me not knowing anything of the rudiments of music or anything like that, and not really desiring to learn them. It's been amazing how we hit it off.

Jimmy Page: It really pissed me off when people compared our first album to The Jeff Beck Group and said it was very close conceptually. It was nonsense. Utter nonsense. The only similarity was that we'd both come out of The Yardbirds and we had both acquired certain riffs individually from The Yardbirds.

Led Zeppelin 2

Jimmy Page: The album took such a long time to make . . . it was all on and off. It was quite insane really. We had no time and we had to write numbers in hotel rooms. By the time the album came out, I was really fed up with it. I'd just heard it so many times in so many places. I really think I lost confidence in it. Even though people were saying it was great, I wasn't convinced myself.

We've been so busy that we just weren't able to go into one studio and polish the album off. It's become ridiculous. We put a rhythm track down in London, add the voice in New York, overdub harmonica in Vancouver and then come back to New York to be here at A&R.

I do worry that the second album is turning out so different from the first. We may have overstepped the mark. But then again, I suppose there are enough Led Zeppelin trademarks in there. It's very hard rock, no doubt about that. There aren't many bands into hard rock these days and I think that might account for some of our success. All sorts of people are into folk, country and soft stuff. We just like to play it hard and bluesy.

Robert Plant: No matter what the critics said, the proof of the pudding was that it got a lot of people off. The reviewer for 'Rolling Stone', for instance, was just a

frustrated musician. Maybe I'm just flying my own little ego ship, but sometimes people seem to resent talent. I don't even remember what the criticism was, but as far as I'm concerned it was a good, maybe even great road album.

'Whole Lotta Love' is something that I personally need, something I just have to have. We bottle it all up, and when we go on stage we can let it all pour out. The song is very good for us. I suppose in a way it's become a Zeppelin cliché, but it's also a vehicle to other things . . . to give people the chance of hearing things that we reckon are worth hearing.

With things like 'Ramble On' and 'Thank You' we are definitely deviating from the original Zeppelin intensity, but without losing any quality. I think we've probably gained quality, because my voice is being used in different ways instead of confining it to a good, safe formula. I think the open chord sort of thing, like Neil Young also uses, is beautiful. I'm obsessed with that kind of music, particularly when it has really good lyrics . . . intense lyrics. What I want is to sit down and write songs and say to the rest of the band: 'Listen to this'.

Led Zeppelin 3

Jimmy Page: We'd been working solidly and thought it was time to have a holiday, or at least to get some time away from the road. Robert suggested going to this cottage in South Wales that he'd once been to with his parents when he was much younger. He was going on about what a beautiful place it was and I became pretty

keen to go there. I'd never spent any time at all in Wales, but I wanted to. So off we went, taking along our guitars of course. It wasn't a question of 'Let's go and knock off a few songs in the country'. It was just a case of wanting to get away for a bit and have a good time. We took along a couple of our roadies and spent the evenings around log fires, with pokers being plunged into cider and that sort of thing. As the nights wore on, the guitars came out and numbers were being written. It wasn't really planned as a working holiday, but some songs did come out of it.

I feel that the new album is perhaps our most significant of all. We're not changing our policy. It wouldn't be fair if we just *completely* changed our sound and announced we were going to do all new things. On the new album we'll be including some quieter acoustic numbers. But we're still a heavy band. We can always infiltrate new material in with our older songs, without making everything from the past seem obsolete.

Robert Plant: You can just see the headlines, can't you? *'LZ go soft on their fans'* or some crap like that. The point is that when you begin a new album, you don't know what you'll come up with that might be different. When we conceived the initial numbers at Bron-y-Aur, we started to see what we wanted this album to do. From the start it was obvious it was going to work, and it just grew from there.

I don't think we'll go into a decline just because we've got into some different things. We've already made people aware of us and what we've got to do now is to consider the position that we've arrived at . . . so that eventually we'll be able to say what we really want to say, and people will listen to it because it's us.

You see, here I am, the lead singer with Led Zeppelin, and underneath I still enjoy people like Fairport Convention and The Buffalo Springfield. Some people may find that surprising. To tell the truth, I've always wanted to go into the realm of that sort of music to a certain degree, without losing the original Zeppelin thing. Some people may have gotten the impression that

I had some unfulfilled ambitions while the last two albums were getting done, but all I can say is that this album is really getting there.

Jimmy Page: When the third LP came out and got its reviews, Crosby, Stills and Nash had just formed. That LP had just come out and because acoustic guitars had come to the forefront all of a sudden: *Led Zeppelin go acoustic!* I thought, Christ, where are their heads and ears? There were three acoustic guitar tracks on the first album, and two on the second.

I think there was a lot of general maturity that was showing by the third album and which a lot of people haven't been able to come to terms with. For me, the third album was very, very good and still had more of an attack than anything before. But obviously people have this preconceived notion of what to expect.

When a band is constantly in a state of change – and that doesn't mean a lack of direction, but natural change – then some people can't come to terms with it, because each album is different. How they should approach our albums is to forget they ever heard of a band called Led Zeppelin, forget about what they expect to hear and just listen to what's on that particular record.

Robert Plant: 'Bron-y-Aur Stomp' was my influence, really. I love folksy things, especially with a beat like that. I don't know if we'll do these numbers on stage. I'm sure the audience wouldn't mind – it depends if they let me play guitar. I didn't play on the album and I'm not very good, but I've been playing the odd rhythm things. I mean, I could never compete with Page.

Jimmy Page: I first heard it ('Gallows Pole') on an old Folkways LP by Fred Gerlach, a 12-string player who was, I believe, the first white to play the instrument. I used his version as a basis and completely changed the arrangement.

Robert Plant: Me and Pagey just sat in the studio at Headley Grange and played through some distorted machines and said 'Hats off to Roy Harper' along with all of the roadies up the back singing 'Yeah' and

banging tambourines. When we played it for Harper, he didn't know what to say. But his time will come—I personally think Roy Harper is one of the best spokesmen this generation has. Despite the subsequent confusion of critics who somehow misconstrued the meaning and thought it was some kind of put-down, 'Hats Off To (Roy) Harper' is just an acknowledgement of a friendship.

I am a reflection of what I sing. Sometimes I have to get serious because the things I've been through are serious. We've been to America so much and seen so many things that we don't agree with, that our feelings of protest have to reflect in our music. When you have the justification, it must be done.

I believe that America makes you aware of the proximity of man's fate. You see so much that is great, but so much that is terrible. The rush, the hassles, the police, you know . . . people may say we make a lot of bread, but in some cities it's so rough

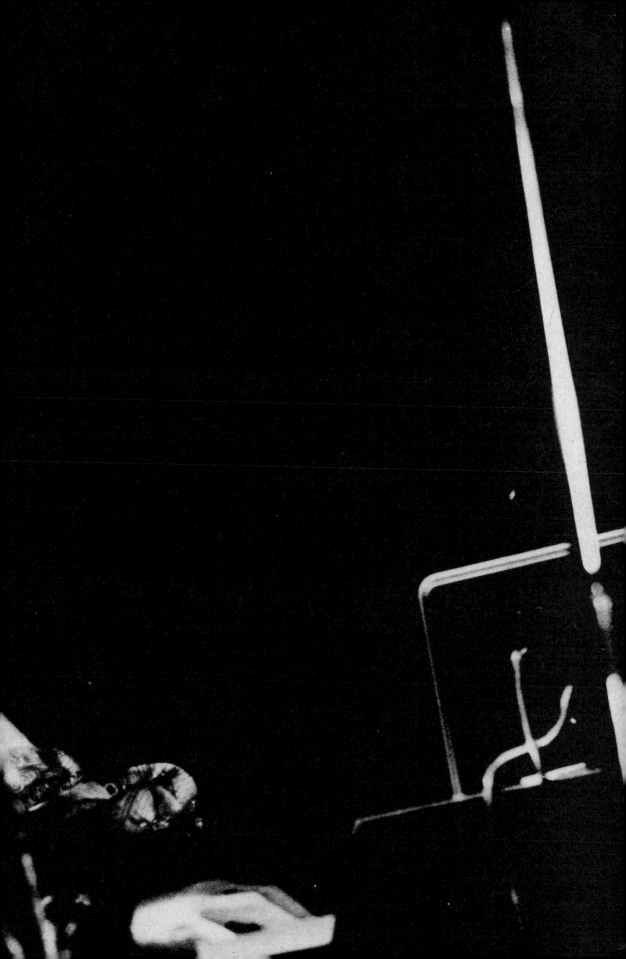

that people are scared to come to our concerts. Our manager once had a gun pulled on him, and we've been threatened with arrest if we returned to the stage for an encore. The police even accused us of being drug addicts. That's all part of where 'That's The Way' came from.

Jimmy Page: The sleeve was intended to be something like one of those garden calendars or the zoo wheel things that tell you when to plant cauliflowers or how long whales are pregnant. But there was some misunderstanding with the artist – who in fact is very good, but had not been correctly briefed – and we ended up on top of a deadline with a teeny-boppish cover which I think was a compromise.

Robert Plant: Now we've done 'Zeppelin III', the sky's the limit. It shows we can change, shows we can do these things. It means there are endless possibilities and directions for us to go in. We're not stale and this proves it.

Led Zeppelin 4 (Four symbols)

Jimmy Page: We started off doing some tracks at the new Island studios in London in December '70, but after that we went to our house, Headley Grange in Hampshire, a place where we frequently rehearse. For some reason, we decided to take the Stones mobile truck there . . . because we were

used to the place. It was familiar territory. We had even lived there during long rehearsal sessions. It seemed ideal – as soon as we thought of an idea, we put it down on tape. In a way, it was a good method. The only thing wrong was that we'd get so excited about an idea that we'd really rush to finish its format to get it on tape. It was like a quick productivity thing. It was just so exciting to have all the facilities there.

Robert Plant: Most of the mood for this new album was brought about in settings that we hadn't come across before. We were living in this old falling-apart mansion way out in the country. The mood was incredible. We could put something down on the spot and hear the results immediately. There was no waiting around until you could get into the studio.

Jimmy Page: We decided that on the fourth album we would deliberately play down the group name, and there wouldn't be any information whatsoever on the outer jacket. Names, titles and things like that do not mean a thing. What does Led Zeppelin mean? It doesn't mean a thing. What matters is our music. If we weren't playing good music, nobody would care what we called ourselves. If the music was good we could call ourselves The Cabbage and still get across to our audience. The words Led Zeppelin do not occur anywhere on this cover. And all the other usual credits are missing too. I had to talk like hell to get that done . . . the record company told us we were committing professional suicide. We said we just wanted to rely purely on the music.

The old man on the cover, carrying the wood, is in harmony with nature. He takes from nature and gives back to the land. It's a natural circle. It's right. His old cottage gets pulled down and they put him in slums – old slums, terrible places. The old man is also the Hermit of the Tarot cards – a symbol of self-reliance and mystical wisdom.

Unfortunately the negatives were a bit duff so you can't quite read an Oxfam poster on the side of a building on the back of the jacket. It's the poster where someone is

lying dead on a stretcher and it says that everyday someone receives relief from hunger. You can just make it out on the jacket if you've seen the poster before. But other than that, there's no writing on the jacket at all.

Robert Plant: We decided the album couldn't be called 'Led Zeppelin IV' and we were wondering what it should be. Then each of us decided to go away and choose a metaphysical type symbol which somehow represented each of us individually – be it a state of mind, an opinion, or something we felt strongly about, or whatever. Then we were to come back together and present our symbols.

My symbol was drawn from sacred symbols of the ancient Mu civilisation which existed about 15,000 years ago as part of a lost continent somewhere in the Pacific Ocean between China and Mexico. All sorts of things can be tied in with Mu civilisation – even the Easter Island effigies. These Mu people left stone tablets with their symbols inscribed into them all over the place . . . in Mexico, Egypt,

Ethiopia, India, China and other places. And they all date from the same time period. The Chinese say these people came from the east and the Mexicans say they came from the west . . . obviously it was somewhere in between. My personal symbol does have a further meaning, and all I can suggest is that people look it up in a suitable reference work.

Jimmy Page: John Paul Jones' symbol, the second from the left, was found in a book about runes and was said to represent a person who is both confident and competent, because it was difficult to draw accurately. Bonzo's came from the same book – he just picked it out because he liked it.

Robert Plant: I suppose it's (Bonzo's symbol) the trilogy – man, woman and child. I suspect it has something to do with the mainstay of all people's beliefs. At one point, though, in Pittsburgh I think, we observed that it was also the emblem of Ballantine beer.

You may not believe this, but Pagey once took me aside and said 'Look, I'm going to

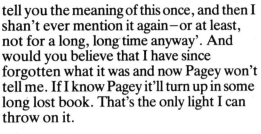

tell you the meaning of this once, and then I shan't ever mention it again – or at least, not for a long, long time anyway'. And would you believe that I have since forgotten what it was and now Pagey won't tell me. If I know Pagey it'll turn up in some long lost book. That's the only light I can throw on it.

We were disgusted at the amount of time it had taken to get the album finished. The sound of the mixing room that Andy Johns, a producer of some note, took Jimmy to was really duff . . . Then there was a hold-up about the pressings, worrying whether they were okay or whether the masters would stand up to how many pressings.

Jimmy Page: 'The Battle Of Evermore' . . . um, I forget whether people had gone to bed early or what, but it just came out then. I picked up the mandolin, which was actually John Paul Jones' mandolin, and those chords just came out. It was my first experiment with mandolin. I suppose all mandolin players would have a great laugh, 'cos it must be the standard thing to play those chords, you know, but possibly not that approach. Anyway, it was just one of those things where I was governed by the limitations of the instrument. Possibly, afterwards, it sounded like a dance-around-the-maypole number I must admit, but it wasn't purposely like that – 'Let's do a folksy number'.

Robert Plant: I'd been reading a book on the Scottish wars just before going to Headley Grange. The number ('Battle Of Evermore') is really more of a playlet than a song. After I wrote the lyrics, I realised that I needed another completely different voice as well as my own to give the song its full impact. So I asked Sandy Denny to come along and sing on the track. I must say I found it very satisfying to sing with someone who has a completely different style to my own. So while I sang about the events in the song, Sandy answered back as if she was the pulse of the people on the battlements. Sandy was playing the role of the town crier, urging people to throw down their weapons.

Jimmy Page: 'Rock 'n' Roll' was a spontaneous combustion. We were doing something else at the time, but Bonzo played the beginning of Little Richard's 'Good Golly Miss Molly' with the tape still running and I just started doing that part of the riff. It actually ground to a halt after about twelve bars, but it was enough to know that there was enough there as a number to keep working on it. Robert even came in singing on it straight away.

To me, I thought 'Stairway' crystallized the essence of the band. It had everything there and showed the band at its best . . . as a band, as a unit. Not talking about solos or anything, it had everything there. We were careful never to release it as a single. It was a milestone for us. Every musician wants to do something of lasting quality, something that will hold up for long time and I guess we did it with 'Stairway'. Townshend probably thought that he got it with 'Tommy'. I don't know whether I have the ability to come up with more. I have to do a lot of hard work before I can get anywhere near those stages of consistent, total brilliance.

Houses Of The Holy

Jimmy Page: I'm happy about that because there's a hell of a lot in that LP. It's not very easy one-time listening, and that's good. You've got to sit down and listen, think about a few things. We can't allow

ourselves the luxury of becoming fascinated with our own popularity. The way I look at it, if The Beatles were to get back together, they would forget all about us.

They just couldn't seem to get it (the sleeve) right at the printers. The colours were so different from what we had anticipated. The basic thing is a photograph in a collage, and then some hand painting . . . we had to compromise because the sky started to look like an ad for Max Factor lipstick, and the children looked as if they'd been turned purple from the cold.

Robert Plant: Every time I sing the song ('The Song Remains The Same'), I picture the fact that I've been round and round the world, and at the root of it all there's a common denominator for everybody. The common denominator is just what makes it good or bad – whether it's Led Zeppelin or Alice Cooper. I'm proud of the lyrics . . . somebody pushed my pen for me, I think. There are lots of catalysts which really bring out these sorts of things . . . working with the group on the road, living where I live, having the friends I've got, my children, my animals.

'D'Yer Maker' was one that just came together straight away at Stargroves, even the creamy vocals. Other times we would have backing track tapes worked out and somebody would say 'We've got no bloody lyrics'. Some of the tapes would be quite intricate and I couldn't sing along instantly. So I had to take them away and listen to them on my own. Then a week later I'd come back with 'Over The Hills' or 'The Crunge'.
    'The Crunge' was amazing, because Bonzo and I were just going into the studio and talking Black Country through the whole thing. You know, 'Bloody hell, how you doin', you all right mate' sort of thing. And it just evolved then and there, when I was at the end of my tether. It just came out.

Jimmy Page: 'The Crunge' just happened spontaneously. Bonzo started playing, Jonesy came in next and then I joined in. It happened as quickly as that. At the time it

seemed to be undanceable, because it keeps crossing over from the on to the off beat, as opposed to most James Brown things which are totally danceable. That's why we called it 'The Crunge'. We thought of putting steps on the cover to help you do the dance.

Physical Graffiti

Jimmy Page: As usual, we had more material than the required 40-odd minutes for one album. We had enough material for one and a half LPs, so we figured let's put out a double and use some of the material we had done previously but never released. It seemed like a good time to do that sort of thing, release tracks like 'Boogie With Stu', which we wouldn't normally be able to do.

'Black Country Woman' and 'Rover' were both done at the same time as we did 'D'Yer Maker'. 'Bron-y-Aur' was done for 'Zeppelin III'. 'Down By The Seaside' and 'Night Flight' and 'Boogie With Stu' were from the sessions for the fourth album.

I came up with that title because of the whole thing of graffiti on the album cover and it being a physical statement rather than a written one, because I feel that an awful lot of physical energy is used in producing an album.

Robert Plant: Let me tell you a little story behind the song 'Ten Years Gone'. I was working my ass off before joining

Zeppelin. A lady I really dearly loved said 'Right, it's me or your fans'. Not that I had fans. But I said 'I can't stop, I've got to keep going'. She's quite content these days, I imagine. She's got a washing machine that works by itself and a little sports car. We wouldn't have anything to say any more. I could probably relate to her, but she couldn't relate to me. I'd be smiling too much. Ten years gone, I'm afraid.

Presence

Robert Plant: 'Presence' was our stand against everything. Our stand against the Elements, against Chance. We were literally fighting against Existence itself. We'd left home for twelve months and it seemed that everything was about to crumble.

Jimmy Page: It was recorded while the group was on the move, technological gypsies. No base, no home. All you could relate to was a new horizon and a suitcase. So there's a lot of movement and aggression. A lot of bad feeling towards being put in that situation.

For that album we all agreed that we'd go right back to square one. Start with nothing . . . just a few basic structures and the minimum of rehearsal. We completed the album in less than two weeks. That's why 'Presence' was a testament . . . if you like, two fingers to all the kinds of things that

destroy other bands. We needed to do that album in so much as we had been together a long time and that we required the challenge of working fast and simply.

There may have been a few ideas on cassette from our travels, but that was all. Everything just came pouring out in the studio and we never came out of a day's playing with long faces, because we always accomplished something. Once we start we just gel.

Robert Plant: As soon as we were familiar with the machinery and the equipment, we were off. I think we only went out twice. We were really too tired to do anything but put our heads down. It was like fourteen hours a day for eighteen days. Jimmy worked like a Trojan. It's his energy that got the album together so quickly. I mean, I was not really in any physical condition to hop around with gusto, inspiring the situation . . . although I was surprised the vocals were so good.

I was sitting at rehearsals in a big, soft, fuckin' armchair, rocking along – facing the group in a fuckin' soft armchair! I mean, if you want to feel really stupid or totally out of it, sing with Led Zeppelin sitting in an armchair. In the end they got me a large stool and every time I really started hitting the notes, I'd sort of raise myself off the stool on one leg and do a Rudolph Nureyev.

The lyrics were all reflections on the time near and before the accident and that time afterwards, that contemplative thing, so I was very determined lyrically and vocally, but Jimmy put his energy into it. He worked so hard, and the guitar playing on this album surpasses anything I've heard for ages and ages. Brilliant . . . so much life in it.

Jimmy Page: I think it was just a reflection of the total anxiety and emotion at the period of time during which it was recorded. It's true that there are no

acoustic songs, no mellowness or contrasts, or changes to other instruments.

Robert Plant: Alone of all the albums we've recorded, 'Presence' relates specifically to a point in time. 'Presence' isn't a précis on Aspects of Life in General, but aspects of hurt. That's what songs like 'Tea For One' and 'Hots On For Nowhere' are all about.

Jimmy Page: I think 'Presence' was a highly underrated record. 'Presence' was pure anxiety and emotion. I mean, we didn't know if we'd ever be able to play in the same way again. It might have been a very dramatic change, if the worst had happened to Robert. 'Presence' is our best in terms of uninterrupted emotion.

The way the cover came about was that after we'd returned from the recording, we realised that the only feasible thing to do was to take a picture of the studio and its chaos, but we needed something better than that, so we contacted Hipgnosis and explained to the chap there, what had been going on.

He returned and said that the thing that had always struck him about Led Zeppelin was a power, a force, an alchemical quality which was indefinable, which I guess he was relating to the magnitude of the band. He came up with this idea of interpreting this through an object which could be related to any object in a community that everyone was perfectly at home with.

The Song Remains The Same

Jimmy Page: We didn't just want the film to be an in-concert type of thing, it had to have bigger dimensions. In America they have a lot of stereo broadcasts linked with TV concerts, so with the film we had to have more than just the sound to capture the imagination.

It was like when we chose a symbol for the fourth album. We each went away and came up with an idea. It gave an insight into each personality, whether it be tongue-in-cheek or deadly serious.

For a time the movie was shelved, and we were going to come over here (America) with what we'd learned and do some more footage. But after Robert's accident we were forced to tie it all up. We'd done work with it already and it had to come out.

I think the film world is fascinating, certainly more on the musical aspect than actually being a character. It hadn't occurred to me, when I was scrambling up the mountain, that I'd have to do about half a dozen takes. Suddenly it hit me that I'd bitten off more than I could chew. In the film it didn't look anywhere near the distance covered – it looked like I was having a promenade.

'The Song Remains The Same' was a live album, but it wasn't *the* best performance, it was just the one that happened to have

celluloid with it. And there are loads of howling guitar mistakes on it. Normally one would be inclined to cut them out, but you can't when it's a soundtrack. It's an honest album in its own way, but a chronological live album is something I've always fancied.

We had two premières in America, one in New York and one in LA. They held them apart by a few days so we could check the cinemas out. It's not as easy a job as you'd think getting the sound right for cinemas. I remember seeing 'Woodstock' and they had towers of speakers.

Well, the first time in New York was great, the first time one had sat in an audience. Every time I had seen the film before was with technicians, people with a really critical eye. Then the film really lived for the first time and you could see people getting off on things, applauding and laughing at the right times, generally vibing.

Peter Grant: The most expensive home movie ever made.

In Through The Out Door

Robert Plant: Abba were very kind and they said 'Why don't you come over and have a look at the studios' (Polar Studios in Stockholm), because they reckoned it was really hot and . . . it's sort of a weird place to go, Sweden. I mean, if you've got any

choice at all I think you might choose other alternatives. Like LA's got pretty good conducive mood for making raunchy records, although everybody seems to come out of there halfway on their knees by the end of studio time. But to trek to Sweden, in the middle of winter, a studio had to be good—and it was, it was sensational and had just the amount of live sound we like.

Normally, a regimental attitude has to be taken in the studio, but with Abba's studio it was very easy-going and the whole series of rooms beckoned for you to play good stuff and dictated the mood, along with the Swedish beer . . . they've got special homes for the people who drink it out there because they go loony after about three weeks—and that's how long it took us to make the album.

Music

In Concert

Jimmy Page: The music of the streets has been returned whence it came. Ours is the folk music of the technological age. The sub-culture. So, as an event, the group is only as good as its audience.

Robert Plant: Without the audience throwing back vibrations, I just couldn't do it. I could not extend myself. When we're on stage and you're looking out into those thousands of faces, it just seems to pour out of me. By allowing your mind to be free and open, you get a new dimension going and the audience comes back at us. I suspect that you could put a lot of the group's success down to that. We've never had the attitude of going out on stage, playing like clockwork for the allotted time and then pissing off. That's not our trip at all.

John Paul Jones: Even now I don't get bored playing on stage with the band. I don't mind being in the background. I wouldn't like to be out front playing like Jimmy. To be any sort or artist you have to be a born exhibitionist. I am, but not over anyone else in the business. I believe you should do what you have to do. If I'm bass, rather than try to lead on bass and push myself, I prefer to put down a good, solid bass line.

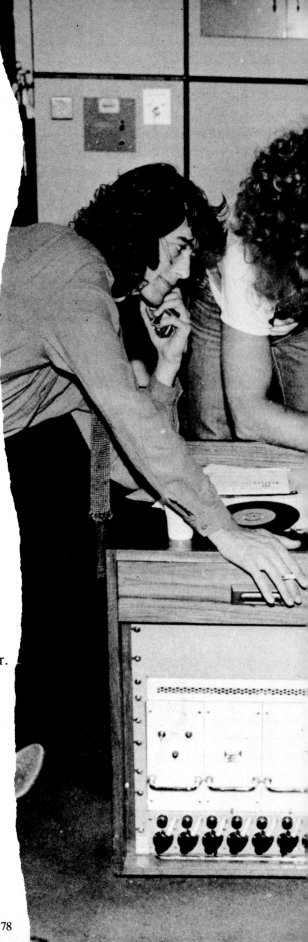

John Bonham: I really like to yell out when I'm playing. I yell like a bear to give it a boost. I like our act to be like a thunderstorm.

Jimmy Page: I think if you've got a set that's cut-and-dried, so well rehearsed that you've no other option but to play it note-for-note each night, then it's bound to get stagnant. We've always structured things so there's an element in which we can suddenly shoot off on something entirely different and see what's happening. Personally speaking, for me, that's where the element of change and surprise comes in . . . the possibilities of having that kind of freedom, should you require it, right in the middle of a number.

John Bonham: We enjoy playing. Every gig is important to us. In this business it doesn't matter how big you are, you can't afford to become complacent. If you adopt that attitude, you're dead. That'll never happen to us.

Jimmy Page: We're very fortunate in that people are prepared to listen to whatever we want to do, without going berserk about old favourites. They don't yell out for 'Whole Lotta Love' before we've finished the second number. Obviously, if we're going to play a three-hour show, we're going to play 'Whole Lotta Love' still because it hasn't become sterile and we still enjoy it as much as the audiences. It's never the same from one night to the next, and it provides the basic framework for us to create some new spontaneous music. You can't disappoint your audience by not playing any of the songs they expect to hear. I think it's selfish to play all new material and expect them to identify with it.

John Bonham: There are some bands who tour America as many times as possible, but although we could do this, the result would be that the audience would go along for the sake of going to a concert and not because it's an event. Before long your prestige goes and you burn yourself out. You must create your own demand.

Robert Plant: There's only one way a band can function, and that's on the bloody stage.

78

In the Studio

John Paul Jones: I would like to think that if we have to stop actually touring, we'll still be in a position to make records together, because this particular combination of people turns out nice things. I've been around long enough to know that very few combinations of people actually work.

Jimmy Page: When I'm in the studio I miss the rapport you get with a live audience. There's only a few people there looking at you through a window. It's all very depressing really. The hardest thing in the world is to get excitement on to a piece of plastic. I really do think everyone plays better on stage than on record.

You really do need the sort of facilities where you can take a break for a cup of tea and wander around the garden, and then go back in and do whatever you have to do.

Instead of all that walking into a studio, down a flight of steps into fluorescent lights and opening up the big sound-proofed door and being surrounded by acoustic tiles. To work like that you've got to programme yourself. You're walking down the stairs telling yourself you're going to play the solo of your life . . . and you so rarely do in those conditions. It's the hospital atmosphere that studios have.

Personally, I get terrible studio nerves. Even when I've worked the whole thing out beforehand at home. I get terribly nervous playing anyway . . . particularly when I've worked on something that proved to be a little above my normal capabilities. When it comes to playing it again in the studio, my bottle goes. It's the studio nerves . . . you never lose them. I might as well be back there years ago making all those dreadful studio records.

John Bonham: Usually we do all the tracks

live to the extent that on some of the album we've also put down live vocals. The only overdubs you're going to get are, say, an extra vocal line, tambourine, lots of percussion and guitar solos, but that's about as far as it goes.

We don't do what a lot of groups do, record each instrument separately, as I feel you lose the atmosphere of the song that way. Getting the instrumental track down as soon as possible enables you to retain the immediacy and energy. Otherwise you're in the studio for a few hours playing the same thing over and over, and you find the track starts sounding uninteresting.

The most we ever do is four takes, and we'll probably decide on the first or second because the feel was probably better.

In the making

Robert Plant: If we roll up somewhere with amps and guitars, then we make electric music. But if we roll up to the farm with acoustic guitars, that's something else and that's when the acoustic stuff gets written.

Jimmy Page: It's just a chord or riff that inspires me and then I go on and see how it goes colour-wise. The whole thing just grows like an acorn or something. I'm not a natural musician, I really have to practise damned hard to get anything out.

Robert Plant: I know in my own mind if I'm satisfied with the way the music and lyrics go together. But the full effect of it often doesn't come through for a long while. It does take quite a long time before you can sit down and hear it the way it really is. Of course, being so close to it doesn't help.

But the fact remains that it's hard to get any distance, not for a while at least. How critics make instant appraisals is beyond me. If it takes me three months to properly appreciate one Zep track, how can critics hope to feel a whole album in a couple of playings?

Jimmy Page: I never felt all that confident about my own lyrics and I was hoping Robert could do all that side, which I think developed from this track ('Thank You').

I contributed lyrics on the first three LPs. After 'Stairway' I realised he'd come such a long way on his level, and everyone else was improving on their level, I thought I'd just concentrate on what I was doing. I've had lyric books and lost them, so it's just like the writing on the wall. And why not? Robert writes damn good lyrics.

I concentrate on the music and stay back from the lyrics. Like 'Ten Years Gone' was originally going to be an instrumental and it has a certain feeling to it, a melancholy feeling, and the theme the lyrics took was exactly along the lines I had been thinking as I had been putting it together.

Robert is very much in sympathy with the vibe of my music. There's a certain amount of discussion, but it's usually just there naturally. I'm sure I could write down on a piece of paper how I visualised a piece of music, before Robert writes the lyrics, and they would match up.

Robert Plant: I spend so much time trying to perfect lyrics that I'd really like to have a book beautifully bound of my really beautiful words. I consider that far more important than breaking the continuity to rush down and do the odd interview.

Jimmy Page: That's what really upsets me about rock. All the barriers are opened up, all the classification is gone really, and you'll find people amalgamating this that and the other music together, and yet there doesn't seem to be anything that's really important without being pretentious. All those really strong melodies like Wagner's—there just isn't anybody. So maybe it's just destined to be street music and social comment. Which makes it art because an artist is somebody who reflects his environment.

The only time I feel—oh no, I won't say the only time—but you know I get very enthusiastic and excited over something that's been written out of nowhere. If your work's going well, everything's fantastic, but if it isn't, you seem to be up against the wall. Obviously there are lots of things one has to come up against which you really hate, but I could never retire because it's so fascinating. You never know what's coming next. It's a challenge. A mystery. It's like dancing on the edge of a precipice.

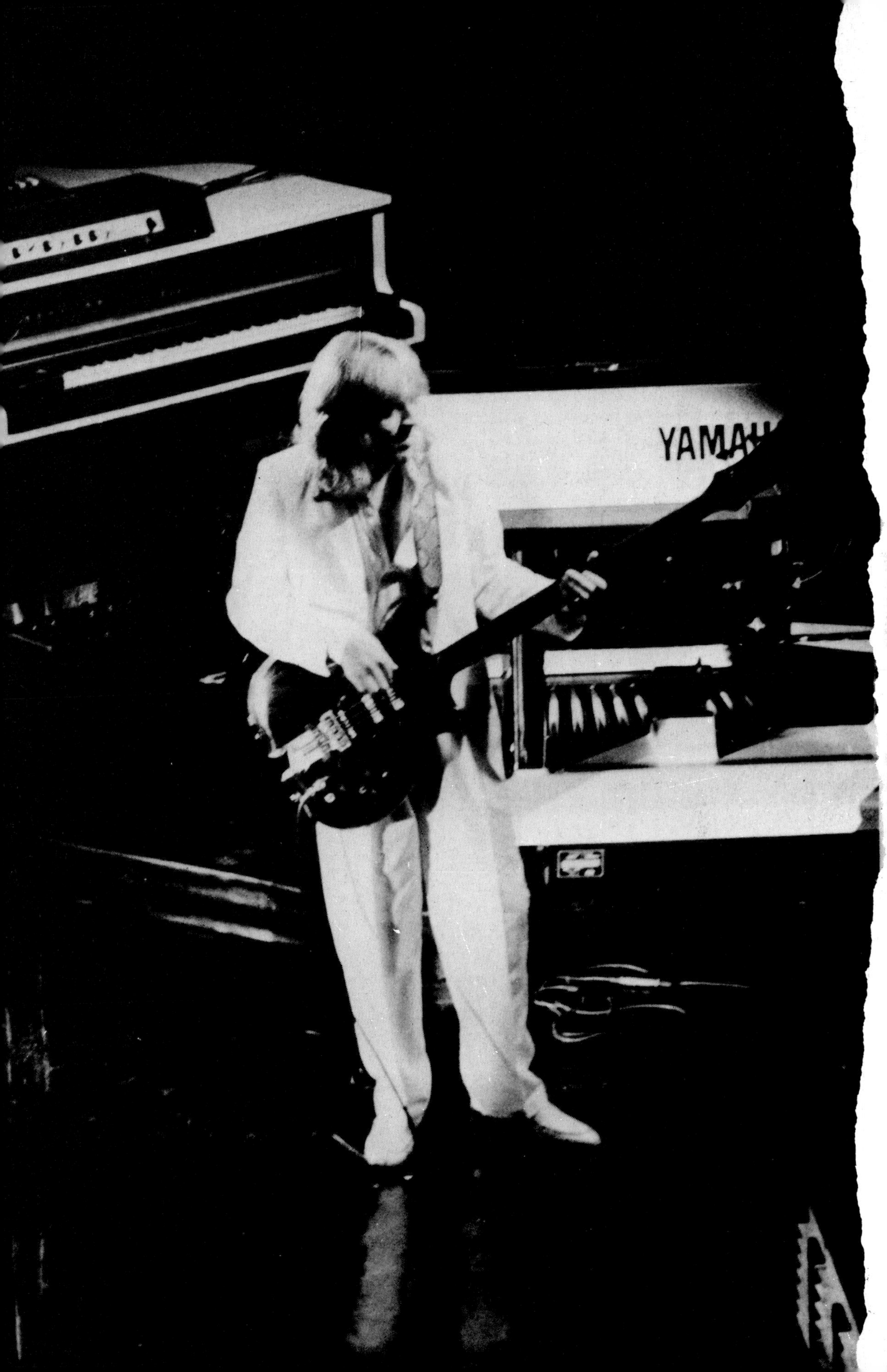
YAMAH

Instruments

John Bonham: People hadn't really taken much notice of drums before Krupa. And Ginger Baker was responsible for the same thing in rock. Rock music had been around for a few years before Baker, but he was the first to come out with this 'new' attitude – that a drummer could be a forward musician in a rock band, and not something that was stuck in the background and forgotten about. I don't think anyone can ever put Ginger Baker down.

Of course, everyone has their own idea of when Baker was at his peak. I thought he was fantastic when he played with the Graham Bond Organization. It's a pity American audiences didn't see that band, because it really was a fantastic group – Ginger Baker, Jack Bruce and Graham Bond.

I think Baker was really more into jazz than rock. He does play with a jazz influence. He's always doing things in 5/4 and 3/4 tempos. Unfortunately he's always been a very weird sort of bloke. You can't really get to know him . . . he just won't allow it. Ginger's thing as a drummer is that he was always himself.

When I started playing I was most impressed by those early soul records. I liked the feel and the sound they achieved . . . and I suppose I said to myself 'I'll get that sound too'. I've always liked drums to be big and powerful. I've never used cymbals much. I use them to crash into a solo and out of it, but basically I prefer the actual drum sound.

I was always breaking drum heads when I first started playing. Later on I learned how to play louder but without hitting the drums so hard. It's all to do with swing. I never had any lessons. When I first started playing I was very interested in music and was able to read it. But when I moved into playing with groups I did a silly thing and dropped it. I do think it's great if you can write ideas down in music form.

But I also think that feeling is a lot more important in drumming than technique. It's all very well to be playing a triple paradiddle – but who's going to know if you're actually doing it. If you pay too much attention to technique you sound like every other drummer does. I think that being original is what counts.

John Paul Jones: Organ, in fact, was always my first love, but for session playing I found it much easier to carry a bass guitar to work than a Hammond organ. So there I was, living with all I had, a guitar, a Hammond organ, a table and a bed in my room.

Robert Plant: You get off an air-conditioned plane into staggering heat. Then into an air-conditioned bar and then back into the heat. Then the air-conditioned hotel. That can affect your voice, especially in dry places with no humidity like Arizona and Texas. I almost got nodes on my vocal chords in Texas, but what can you do? All singers have to worry about that, but you still can't restrain yourself. You can't walk out on stage and say 'OK, chaps, you'll have to change key tonight because I can't cope'.

I don't know how my voice stands up to it, particularly on long tours of the States with the flying and changes of conditions. It's like waking up croaky in the morning, and the only solution seems to be lemon and honey. Either that or I've got a cast-iron vocal case.

Jimmy Page: My first guitar worth talking about was a Stratocaster. Then I had something called a Grazioso – don't know where it came from. It was probably a Czechoslovakian version of Fender. That's what it looked like, anyway. Then I got a Fender Strat, then something very similar to that but a later model.

The company were making patented pick-ups at that time, though I had that for five years. Yeah, I played that with The Crusaders. Then I got a Les Paul Custom which I stayed with until it was nicked in the States during the first eighteen months of Zeppelin – the second or third tour. Usually I never took that on the road because it was so precious, but things were going so well for us that I eventually took it over and suddenly it went.

It had a big tremolo arm and Jo Jammer counter-wired it for me. I was starting to use it more than anything else. It got nicked off the truck at the airport – we were on our way to Canada. Somewhere there was a flight change and it disappeared. It just never arrived at the other end.

I advertised for it in 'Rolling Stone'. Just a photograph – no name – and a reward. No luck, though, even though it was very recognisable for all the custom work done to it.

Those old guitars made between 1952 and 1960 were made by the last of the post-war craftsmen. I find they're more responsive to the player's touch. Like the old Stratocaster. Eric was probably the first to popularise the use of the Stratocaster with two pick-ups. My favourite was the old Fender Telecaster. Now, of course, you have to be very careful you don't pick up a fake, because the Japanese – and indeed some of the original manufacturers – are now remaking the old models. But without that individual craftsmanship that counted.

I've never broken a guitar, but I've been through nearly every make. I've never found a guitar which is exactly what I want. At the moment I'm happy with the Gibson. I've also got a 1958 Fender Telecaster. I find every guitar's got a sound of its own and you can use them all and get something different out of each of them. I haven't used the Telecaster on stage yet. Actually, all my guitars are in England because I came over playing bass. I switched to Jeff's guitar. (1966)

When I was doing sessions I'd been playing with a violin bow across the strings, which I suppose I could say has become a bit of a trademark now, but that wasn't actually my idea. It was suggested to me by one of the violinists in the string section. It obviously looks a bit gimmicky because one hasn't seen it done before, and as soon as you pick up a bow and start playing guitar with it that's the first thing people say – 'Oh, that's an interesting gimmick' – but the fact is that it's very musical, it sound like an orchestra at times, the cello section, violins . . . it's quite amazing! The only drawback of the technique is that the guitar has a flat neck as opposed to a violin's curved neck, which is a bit limiting.

Lifestyle

Life on the road

Robert Plant: The fact is we don't flog Led Zeppelin to death. Just like John Lennon once said: 'If you're on the road for too long, it becomes painful'.

John Bonham: There are times when you sit down and say 'I wanna go home'. It's not the playing—I could do that all day!—it's the surroundings, and it usually means a loss of weight of half a stone and an adequate supply of Noxema or similar hand lotions to control the numerous blisters.

Robert Plant: Tours are exhausting, no doubt about that. But I think the thing is that when you step off the plane in Heathrow, or wherever, all the exhaustion lifts. I suppose America isn't bad, but it just isn't home. You can be tired and overworked every day at home, but it's okay because it *is* home. That's the difference.

Jimmy Page: I did have a scheme which would cater to this sort of live playing, getting the feedback from the audience and all that. The idea is to get a truck with a drop-down side to make a stage, using battery amplifiers, and just drive through all these little villages. We could stop anywhere, hand out a few circulars and play in the evening.

My thoughts were to play acoustic stuff, that area of playing that I just don't get a chance to manifest, and without all the hubbub that goes on . . . and anybody could come up and play or whatever. It could be really good, a mystery tour, because nobody would know where you were going to play and all the sensationalism, thank God, would be gone.

John Paul Jones: I get hell for going on tour. Once I had all the time in the world and no money. Now I have the money but no time . . .

John Bonham: Sometimes it gets a bit wearing, but that's only because I'm married with kids at home. I've never gotten pissed off with the actual touring. I enjoy playing—I could play every night. It's just the being away that gets you down sometimes. I still enjoy going through different towns we haven't been to before. But you get fed up with places like New York because they're not interesting any more.

Jimmy Page: There are many things about America I like. Things that Americans take for granted, like a good telephone system. And they don't force you to go to bed at 10.30 pm by switching off all the TV programmes and stopping the trains.

John Bonham: The restaurant scene in the South can be unbelievable. We've stopped for a coffee and watched everybody else in the place get service, people who came in after we did. Everybody sits and glares at you, waiting and hoping that you'll explode and a scene will start.

We even had a gun pulled on us in Texas. Some guy was shouting out and giving us general crap about our hair and all, so we simply gave it back to him. We were leaving after the show and this same guy turned up at the door. He pulls out this pistol and says to us 'You guys gonna do any shouting now?'. We cleared out of there tout de suite.

Peter Grant: You know, we were in the Midwest and I said something to the hotel clerk about the fact that it must be tough to have all the rock groups in there throwing

furniture and TVs out the windows, and he said that they had something worse once . . . and that was the Young Methodists Convention. Apparently they threw the carpets and everything out, and this clerk went into the whole rap about 'Well, it's all right for you guys to take out all your things on stuff like that, but how do you think I'd feel, never being able to do the same thing?'. So I jeered him on a bit and said 'You'd really like that wouldn't you?', and he said 'Oh yeah, I'd love to do it'. So I said 'Well, have one on us. I'll treat you. Do whatever you want to do'. And he went in and he fucking threw all the stuff around and threw the stuff out the windows and I went down to the desk and paid his bill . . . $490.

Jimmy Page: I've had brushes with Bill Graham in the past. I'll give you an example. It was the Fillmore where we really broke, and the whole name and news of the group spread like wildfire through the States from there. Obviously on the return we were really excited to be back and wanted to do our best.

Now, when we got there it was in the afternoon and I went in with the road manager, 'cos we wanted to carry the gear in then, and Graham was playing basketball. I remember going up to him—he didn't seem to be doing anything at the time, he seemed like the referee—and I said 'Hi, Bill, it's really good to see you. Can we bring the gear in now?'

And he said 'Don't you fucking get in here, you motherfuckers' and all this real abuse. It was just like he exploded. I was really brought down because we really built ourselves up to going back. Then later he apologised, I mean, he's a pendulum.

I was once informed that someone was set on killing me while I was in the States. Actually, it was a lot more serious than I thought. The guy was a real crazy and had all these photographs on the wall with circles round them. It was a real Manson situation and he was sending out waves of this absurd paranoia which a friend of mine got mixed up with. I got to hear of it through him and actually hired a security guard along for that American tour. It was actually a lot worse than everyone at first

believed, and eventually this guy was tracked down and got carted away to hospital. He would have definitely had a try, though. It's things like that that tend to lessen the effect of having £80,000 ripped off at the end of a successful tour.

Robert Plant: Most of the girls who come backstage simply want to say 'Thank you' to us for giving a good concert. Outsiders who think that all sorts of stuff is going on just don't know us. I'll admit the first year or two that I became a star I was very young and was on a sort of trip. But we've all gotten over that now and we're mostly concerned with our music . . . getting it right.

Jimmy Page: Down there (Texas) they've got the richest groupies in the world. Some of the groupies followed our jet in their private jet.

Robert Plant: You get bored. Anything that's ever happened has been in a spirit of fun. We never hurt anybody. Well, no-one who didn't dig it.

Jimmy Page: It's something you can't really dwell on because people think if you're doing it, then the rest of the band are into it too and that would cause all kinds of trouble. No, it's . . . well, all I can say is that it comes down to the term 'road fever'. I mean, I personally can't play a gig in some God-forsaken part of America to God-knows-how-many people and then return to a box. It's just a total change of lifestyle. That's all one can say, really.

Peter Grant: The thing about sharks is that the best shark bit never got out. There must have been about twenty eight or thirty odd sharks that were caught by the band once, and they stacked them up in the wardrobe closet. So when the maids came in, as they obviously did to check the rooms after we left, they opened the door and an avalanche of sharks came tumbling out.

Robert Plant: Of course, it's usually one of our roadies that rides along with us and then gets us a bad reputation with his shenanigans.

John Paul Jones: Nothing exciting ever happens to me.

Life at home

Jimmy Page: The Americans are a little more narrow-minded. The English, at the moment, are completely broad-minded. You can shock people in America very easily. If people are shocked that's their bad luck. They should open their minds. In England you could walk around in the nude and you wouldn't shock anybody. They'd think you should be put away, but they wouldn't beat the guts out of you.

John Paul Jones: The policemen don't carry guns and they don't start trouble. In the States it seems that police are always starting trouble. In England there hasn't been a war for twenty five years and people are getting a bit restless. They can't really scream at the government because it's only a side-show. British kids can't really get their teeth into anything.

Touring makes you into a different person, I think. You always realise it when you come home after a tour. It usually takes weeks to recover after living like an animal for so long.

Robert Plant: I think marriage for me was the make-or-break of being a stable person, or just going on with this out-and-out looning. In the pop world where everything gets blown up and unreal, you never know what's going to happen. You are going to have children here there and everywhere if you lead that sort of life – and you've got to expect the consequences. I don't often admit it, but being married is part of the peace of mind and stability thing I hope I've found.

(During tax exile.) That little farm of mine is a lot of my life and so are the two little seeds that run around it. If the government could lead a reformation, under reasonable terms, I'd have no qualms about going back and saying 'OK, let's make a deal'. And I know everybody else feels the same. But it's this attitude of 'Gotta get it all, gotta fill me pockets', which is not where I've been at, despite a few rather uneducated people commenting that that is all. So I suppose when I do go home it'll be 'Hallelujah!' and I shall kiss the soil again.

It gives me room to think, to breathe and live. I wake up in the morning and there are no buses and no traffic. Just the sound of the tractors and the odd pheasant shooting in the next field. I'd been around big cities since I first left home and ran away to Walsall. I was pretty fed up with humanity in the big cities. The atmosphere here is just so easy-going. They say the village folk never die . . . they have to be shot. I just revel in these country things. Chickens and goats and me horse. There are Stone Age tools in the garden and a cave. I'm really intrigued by the mixture of romance and reality. After reading Tolkien I just had to have a place in the country.

Aleister Crowley
Jimmy Page: All my houses are isolated. Many is the time I just stay home alone. I spend a lot of time near water. Crowley's house is in Loch Ness, Scotland. There were two or three owners before Crowley moved into it. It was also a church that was burned to the ground with the congregation in it. And that's the site of the house. Strange things have happened in that house that had nothing to do with Crowley. The bad vibes were already there.

I feel he's a misunderstood genius of the twentieth century. Because his whole thing was liberation of the person, of the entity, and that restriction would foul you up, lead to frustration which leads to violence, crime, mental breakdown depending on what sort of make-up you have underneath. The further this age we're in gets into technology and alienation, a lot of the points he made can be seen to manifest themselves all down the line.

His thing was total liberation and really getting down to what part you played. What you want to do, do it. Anyway, that's a minor thing, just one of the things they couldn't come to terms with. Saying there would be equality of the sexes. In an Edwardian age that's just not on. He wasn't necessarily waving a banner, but he knew it was going to happen. He was a visionary and he didn't break them in gently.

I'm not saying it's a system for

anybody to follow. I don't agree with everything but I find a lot of it relevant and it's those things that people attacked him on, so he was misunderstood.

I don't want to go into it too much. I don't want to get like Pete Townshend and Meher Baba because I'm sure most people would find it very boring. I'm not trying to interest anyone in Aleister Crowley any more than I am in Charles Dickens. All it was, was that at a particular time he was expounding a theory of self-liberation, which is something which is so important. He was like an eye to the world, into the forthcoming situation. My studies have been quite intensive, but I don't particularly want to go into it because it's a personal thing and isn't in relation to anything apart from the fact that I've employed his system in my own day-to-day life.

It's the idea of liberation, that man is doing a job and wants to be doing something else, and that suppression of his will—of what he is, is a very sorry state of affairs. It can make a man sick, mentally and physically, or it can manifest itself in other ways—violence or aggression of some form. The thing is to come to terms with one's free will, discover one's place and what one is, and from that you can go ahead and do it and not spend your whole life suppressed and frustrated. It's very basically coming to terms with yourself. That's a very simple account.

And that is the way big names are made these days. Not via the press or 'Ready Steady Go', but by people seeing them and making up their own minds.

Jimmy Page: You can develop a tremendous insecurity if your management isn't totally reliable. I know that money is a dirty word in this business, but the fact remains that if you have any measure of record success, you're going to have royalties coming in. Many groups who have been working for years and years end up with nothing because they've been screwed all the way down the line. That sort of thing is heartbreaking. We're very lucky in that respect because we've got Peter Grant, who is like a fifth member of the group.

Robert Plant: I hate the way people slam us for going to America, saying it's all for the bread. In the old days people used to leave groups if they weren't making money. We have earned our money. We've gone almost a year without a real break. I don't think any fair-minded person would begrudge us.

Jimmy Page: It's not as though I have it all in my hands, building a big bank or something. It all goes away at the moment. The only problem is tax and how much one ends up with when there's about 90% to pay in Britain. It doesn't really come down to much in the end.

John Bonham: (on the theft of $180,000 from the Drake Hotel, New York, 1973.) If we'd have said we were not upset, they would have thought we were so rich it meant nothing to us, and if we say we're upset about it, they'll say money is all we care about.

Peter Grant: Expenses down means profits up.

Robert Plant: People say I'm a millionaire, but that's not true—I only spend millions.

Opinions

Image

Peter Grant: You don't have to be flash any more. The days when agents and managers wore only mohair suits and smoked large cigars are in the past. I'm not a prima donna, I'm a working manager.

Robert Plant: I've been told I'm a 'sexual beacon'.

It seems funny that a few months ago I was an ungratified singer and now they're calling me the next sex symbol. It can't be bad. I must admit that I don't really know how people think about sex symbols. Maybe if the audience can see a cock through a pair of trousers, then that must make you a sex symbol. Since I'm the only one who doesn't have a guitar or drums in front of mine, I suppose I started out with a bit more chance than anyone else in the band. Really you can't take it seriously, simply because you read all these things about it in the papers. You just get into your music and the sexual thing isn't really apparent to you. It's simply not what we're there for.

Jimmy Page: They are talking about Robert Plant as the next Mick Jagger, but we never set out to contrive a big, sexy image . . . it's stupid to base your image on a big sex angle. *Music* is what it's all about today.

Mild barbarians was how we were once described, and I can't really deny it.

I'm no fool. I know how much mystique matters, so why should I blow it now?

Money

Peter Grant: There's a memory I have of the days when I was a tour manager and I'd see these groups and good artists turn up on Friday to collect their week's pay from managers as tough and insensitive as leather. I always felt bad about that, and I said to myself that if I became a manager I would never be like that. That's the main thing – doing the best you can and staying by people whatever happens.

When I took over the management of The Yardbirds, I was advised to get rid of Pagey, their lead guitarist. He was a troublemaker I was told, and I soon found out why. The Yardbirds had recently appeared in Antonioni's 'Blow Up', recorded its title song, then been round the States with The Rolling Stones, done their own US tour for five weeks, and had exactly £112 each to show for it. Someone had ripped them off mightily . . . I vowed it would never happen again.

The days of the promoter giving a few quid to the group as against the money taken on the door is gone. The business was run by managers, agents and promoters when the funny thing about this business is it is the groups who bring the people in.

I thought the musicians who bring people in should be the people who get the wages. Now we take the risks. We pay the rent of the hall, we pay the local supporting groups, we pay the promoter to set it up for us.

Swan Song

Jimmy Page: I had a long acoustic guitar instrumental with just sparse vocal sections – the number was about twenty minutes long and the vocal was about six minutes, and the whole thing was quite epic, really. Almost semi-classical, I suppose, and I had bits of it and we were recording with the truck and there was no title for it and someone shouted out 'What's it going to be called?' and I shouted 'Swan Song', and the whole thing stopped and we said what a great name for the LP. All the vibes started and suddenly it was out of the LP and on to the record label. I think Swansong is a good name for a record label because if you don't have success on Swansong . . . well, you shouldn't have signed up with them.

I'm not personally involved with the business side of it, because I'm so involved with the production of our records that I just can't and don't have time to worry about that side of it, or even take a look at it. There are finer points where the two cross and I get involved then, but apart from that I don't pay much attention to what's going on behind the scenes.

Robert Plant: The label isn't going to be like 'Yeah, we'll have a label, far out heavy trip man' and just put yourself on it sort of trip. The label won't just be Led Zeppelin, that's for sure. It's too much effort to do as an ego trip and a waste of time, really. I haven't got to build myself up on my own label, for Chrissakes.

We're going to work with people we've known and we've liked, and people we will know and will like. It's an outlet for people we admire and want to help. There are so many possible things we can play around with, people we can help that we haven't been able to help before. People like Roy Harper whose records are so good and haven't even been out in America.

We want to take some artists who we think

are fine, and never let them down at any point . . . that's our intention. On so many labels there've been fantastic albums, but they didn't get the stimulation of people involved in the record industry.

Jimmy Page: We'd been thinking about it for a while and we knew that if we formed a label there wouldn't be the kind of fuss and bother we'd been going through over album covers and things like that. Having gone through ourselves what appeared to be an interference or at least an aggravation on the artistic side by record companies, we wanted to form a label where the artists would be able to fulfil themselves without all of that hassle. Consequently, the people we were auditioning for the label would be people who knew where they were going themselves. We didn't really want to get bogged down in having to develop artists, we wanted people who were together enough to handle that type of thing themselves.

There is one awkward situation with the label, which is that a lot of folk come along and seem to think that Peter Grant is going to be able to do everything for them. It's just one of those unfortunate things that he's there and they respect him, but he just doesn't want to know. He's got too much on his plate.

New Wave

Robert Plant: As a basic movement – it's good, but I wish the music was more original and was moving on a stage. The Stranglers, for example, sound like an English Doors pre 'LA Woman'. So that doesn't do much for me or anybody else, really.

The intensity and excitement I do like, because I never forget the first time I saw The Small Faces and The Who when I was at school. It was that very thing that made me go 'Yeah!' – and I rushed to the barber's and got a French crew or whatever they were called, the right mod haircut.

So I know what all that's about, rushing around getting a parka and immediately getting chrome side panels for

your scooter and belonging again, 'cos I was just a bit too young for the drape jackets.

I understand all that. Everyone needs something to hang on to a little bit, on some level of mass entertainment.

Jimmy Page: We were aware of it, but it's not . . . I mean, music is like a 360° circle from which some people may drop out to let others come in. And there are obvious examples of that. Say, the feeling that Free generated and which was replaced by Bad Company. Also, the raw blues, going back to the early Fleetwood Mac days. Well, now you have George Thorogood. And Herman's Hermits are replaced by the Bay City Rollers.

Bands like us and – I hate to say it but . . . The Floyd . . . we're off in our own little bits. It's always open for anybody who's really raw and earthy and who makes sheer rock'n'roll music. Even though much of the New Wave has political content . . . I mean, The Damned – I was absolutely amazed by the power that was coming out of them. Though they didn't really fit into the New Wave movement as such.

Nevertheless, there are categories. But it's all relative. Anyone who plays good music and is expressing themselves with an instrument or vocals has got something to say. It just depends whether you can relate to them or not. And that also depends on whether your musical tastes are narrow or very broad . . . People write to us, you know, and a lot of younger people who I'd never have expected to have got into us have said that they got really fired by the energy of New Wave bands – and they still like New Wave bands – but they got interested in the actual musical content and wanted to go one step further, which is how they discovered bands like us.

The Press

Jimmy Page: This guy came up and got talking to me. He said he was from 'Rock', which is quite an eminent, respected magazine in the States, isn't it? He asked me things like 'Does Plant still gyrate about on stage?' and I said 'Well, if it's a fast number he does move about, yes, but it depends on what we're playing' – and this conversation went on at that sort of level until, bit by bit, from the sort of questions he was asking, it became evident that he didn't really know what he was on about. So I asked him exactly when he'd last seen the band. 'Quite a while ago now', he mumbled, and when I questioned him a bit more it transpired that the only time he'd seen us was in 'Supershow', which was a film made a couple of months after we formed.

So here was a respected critic, who had done reviews of our albums, and he didn't know the first thing about us . . . didn't even know that we played acoustic numbers on stage.

But the thing is, these reviewers are so authoritative. We know they might be twits, but the readers may well believe them because of the eloquent, authoritative way they write. It's so easy to criticise someone's music, but when you think how much thought and care and time it's taken, why not look for the good points at least?

I don't think some of the so-called critics realise just how much they can hurt or affect an artist. It's only quite recently I

have been able to get a proper perspective on their relative significance.

No one would dispute the power of the press en masse, but it's those few individuals trying to make a name for themselves with trite and caustic comments who get through on a personal level.

I've realised now, though, that one or two exceptionally offensive remarks won't harm a group or a career. It would only be serious if the general consensus of opinion was against us.

I know Eric Clapton went through some sort of press paranoia, and so did I. I once adopted the approach of refusing to read the papers and worried only about my music.

The third LP did get a real hammering from the press and I really got brought down by it. I thought the album in total was good. But the press didn't like it, and they also went on about this enigma that has blown up around us. I admit we may have made it relatively quickly, but I don't think we ever overplayed our hand in the press or anything. Yet we were getting all these knocks and we became very dispirited. The result was that we left off for almost a year.

Robert Plant: We decided to hire our first publicity firm after we toured here (America) in the summer of '72. That was the same summer that the Stones toured

and we knew full well that we were doing more business than them. We were getting better gates in comparison to a lot of people who were constantly glorified in the press. So without getting egocentric, we thought it was time people heard something about us other than that we were eating women and throwing the bones out of the window. That whole lunacy thing was all people knew about us and it was all word-of-mouth. All these times of lunacy were OK, but we aren't and never were monsters. Just good-time boys, loved by their fans and hated by their critics.

Jimmy Page: Who wants to know that Led Zeppelin broke an attendance record at such-and-such a place when Mick Jagger's hanging around with Truman Capote?

John Paul Jones: Aww . . . they want to interview the stars, not the rhythm section.

Each other

Peter Grant: Jimmy is known as Led Wallet because he's always got a heavy wallet and it stays in his pocket. Robert has a farm in Worcestershire and lives on it with his goats. John is happy so long as he's got a pint of bitter. He's also had more fast cars than anyone else I know. The Birmingham car dealers could survive on him. John Paul Jones is the antithesis of the pop star. You never see him. He's like a recluse and only comes out when there's a concert to play or an album to make.

Robert Plant: If we had not had Peter behind us we could easily have gone to pieces. As much as the credit goes to us, it goes to Peter, because he went all around the States with us, everywhere we went, when he could have just sat in an office. He's been a big part of the whole thing.

Peter Grant: I have no musical knowledge, but it's purely a feeling thing with me. It's

not just liking the sound you hear, it's a feeling that it's either got the magic or it hasn't. I can't define it, but it works.

Jimmy Page: Well, he's a big guy and if people are coming up to him all the time and calling him a bastard and telling him to piss off to his face, then he's probably going to react accordingly.

There is a very powerful astrological force at work within the band which I am sure had a lot to do with our success. Robert is a Leo which makes him a perfect leader with two Capricorns on either side and a Gemini behind. Leo is always a leader like Ginger Baker, Keith Moon and Mick Jagger. I'm a Capricorn which speaks for itself: very stubborn with a split personality.

John Bonham: We get on well. The whole group gets on well. To me some groups get too close and the slightest thing can upset the whole thing. In this group, we're just close enough. It's never a case of somebody saying something and the whole band being on the verge of breaking up. I think you get more enjoyment out of playing with each

other if you don't know everyone too well. Sometimes it isn't any fun any more to play with a group you've been in for years, but with Led Zeppelin we're always writing new stuff, doing new things and every individual is important and getting into new things.

Robert Plant: It's taken a long time to know each other properly. A lot of the time that we've spent together has been in getting on with what's in hand rather than with getting to know each other. We've got to know each other more through playing than we got to the playing through knowing each other.

John Bonham: I'm still the same person. I enjoy decorating and gardening and I'm still as hot-headed as ever. I'm a bit quick-tempered . . . I never sit down and think about things. I couldn't do what Jimmy does and shut myself away in the country. I like people around me all the time . . . parties, going out and general looning. I suppose I'm a bit of a noisy person. In fact, I'm probably the noisiest of the four of us.

We're pretty easy-going with each other, we don't look for trouble. I don't think that four blokes can live together on their own, like some supergroups go to a cottage to get it together. You've got to be together, but not every hour of the day. If they decided to enjoy each other's music and respect each other, it would work. Everyone in Led Zeppelin is completely different and that helps.

Jimmy Page: There's no reason to split up. There is nothing inherent musically in Led Zeppelin to harm or destroy it. There is variety, great freedom and no restrictions on the players whatsoever. It's good from a head point of view. In our band everybody respects everybody else. Everybody plays something to knock each other out.

I can't see any split coming. People say to us 'Now you're established, when are you going to break up?' That's a terrible attitude.

I heard recently that Crosby, Stills and

Nash are going to split up. Fans develop loyalty to a group and that becomes impossible when groups break up so often. We'll carry on and stick together . . . like The Beatles and the Stones.

Robert Plant: In this band we're very lucky that everybody is more enthusiastic as time goes on. There is not fatigue or boredom musically at all. There's a bit of boredom when you're stuck in Mobile, Alabama or places like that. A few lamp standards may fall out of the windows – things like that – but we move on and we keep playing that music.

Peter Grant: The group will stay intact as long as they're happy making music together. My contribution? To make sure they're protected at all times and make the when-and-where decisions.

Jimmy Page: It would be a criminal act to break up this band.

The Solo Years

Robert Plant

On gigging with The Honeydrippers:

As far as I am concerned there is no more Led Zeppelin. No more Led anything. The band no longer exists. We got together and made the decision to call it a day. This is just a rhythm and blues excuse-me. It takes me back with great pleasure to the early days of my career with The Band Of Joy. The other members of this line-up have their own separate careers in other bands. We just come together to play the clubs when we feel like it.

On making Pictures At Eleven:

Robbie Blunt and I had been playing in The Honeydrippers, playing out our fantasies with R&B. It was enjoyable but gradually we could see the limitations. So in between the gigs we started writing bits and pieces and got them down on a little four track tape machine. Then we went to Rockfield and hooked up with Cozy Powell who did a couple of initial tracks with us. It was all done in fits and starts to avoid spending too much time in the studio to keep it fresh.

When it was finished I actually drove up to see Page at his Sol Studio and played him some tracks. We sat there together with my hand on his knee just listening. It was an emotional time and he knew then I was off on my own.

On the possibility of touring:

I'd like to be able to go onstage and do a complete set of material that features this album and the next one. That would give me about two hours of material and until then there's no point going out on the road. As for the Zeppelin numbers – I love them but I ain't gonna play Zepp numbers without Zeppelin. It's as simple as that. Maybe in the bath, but not for an audience. It would not be right or fair. Those songs belong to that group, not just me.

On making Principle Of Moments:

I think the sound has broadened out a little. There's less vocal and guitar prominence. The keyboards are playing a more important part. Jezz Woodroffe's identity is obviously important because the sound of that record would have been totally different without him.

On scoring a hit with Big Log:

I'm pleased it's done so well. There's a lot of dignity about it. And it was great doing Top Of The Pops. The sort of lack of cool of doing TV shows has gone to the dogs now. I don't want to have an audience that gets smaller and smaller. I want it to expand as the music expands and draw in people with a wider appreciation level. And if that means doing stuff like Top Of The Pops then so be it.

On his first solo tour:

I haven't been this enthusiastic about music for years and years. It's incredibly challenging because a good percentage of people who come to see the show come in out of good faith. They're standard bearers and they know I don't play Zeppelin stuff... but there's always a chance I might crack. I'm sure I could find some snakeskin boots, and I needn't have cut my hair. I could have kept everything as people wanted it. But I'd much rather be associated with the new songs. Maybe 15 or 20 per cent of the audience may never come again because they find this change too radical. But I can blow the whole thing in one second by doing 'Whole Lotta Love' for the encore.

On recording The Honeydrippers' mini album:

It started out as a wild weekend with Ahmet Ertegun coaxing me into singing some of my favourite R&B songs. Then it all got out of hand. It proved to be another fragmentation of my career. It was a great thing to do, but the fact that it eclipsed my solo work pissed me off no end. It sold two million in the States which made me wonder about struggling along singing 'Big Log' when everybody really wanted me to sing Marty Wilde songs. There was not much point in me sounding like an Americanised version of Shakin' Stevens so a volume two was never on the cards.

On making Shaken N' Stirred:

I actually still think it was mostly brilliant. I tried to continue to change at will. If I have a big fad on one area of music I just pursue it. With that album I wanted to do away with the guitar in its natural form. So by using one of those Roland guitar synthesisers, we tried to make so many solos that were not blues based. We were trying to make guitar solos that sounded like signature tunes from some unmade French detective movie from 1961. I was probably going up my own backside a bit in trying to be different.

On forming a new recording and touring unit for Now And Zen:

After three solo albums and two tours I felt that some of us had lost the plot, and the momentum got changed and distorted. I kept trucking along pursuing this kind of very singular aim to create an alternative brand of music that maybe borrows from Led Zeppelin but is primarily me. I guess I wanted to meet the next generation and also find out how what I'd done in the past had affected them. So by working with Phil Johnstone and Doug and Charlie I've found a level that is really vibrant. The music is fresh and new although we are now leaning on the Zeppelin thing. I spent too much time pretending I wasn't the singer in Led Zeppelin. I now realise Led Zeppelin is present tense whether I want it or not.

On performing Led Zeppelin songs as part of his post-1988 touring set:

I guess I am eating a sizeable proportion of my own words. But these are great songs and I think enough time has now lapsed. Some of them are sacred still, but if I want to romp through 'Misty Mountain Hop' again, well it's my prerogative.

On sampling Zepp songs on Now And Zen:

It was a chance to get my own back on The Beastie Boys! I used 'The Ocean' because they used it on 'She's Crafty'. When Jimmy did the solo on 'Tall Call One' I'd yet to layer on the samples. When we played it back to him I wish I'd have had a camera to catch his expression. I wasn't taking the piss. Just showing that these were the mightiest riffs the world has ever heard.

Asking Jimmy to contribute two solos on Now And Zen:

Really, I just wanted my old partner around for a bit. I wanted to see him swaying around, leaning around so his hair was dangling on the floor. Everyone in the control room was going 'God, look at that man play'. I was sitting there feeling very proud.

On making Manic Nirvana:

This is a far more techno sounding record than I've ever done. So far the critics seem to be picking up on the sample of James Brown's 'Cold Sweat' we put in SSS and Q. And there's even a sample from 'Woodstock' on 'Tie Dye On The Highway'. For all the contempt for old hippies, the kids today seem to regret missing it as the high point of youth culture. There's a lot to be gained from re-telling that tale. Bands like The Stone Roses and Happy Mondays are making quite a decent living by harkening back to that period.

On receiving the Silver Clef Award in 1990 and reuniting with Jimmy Page for the Knebworth '90 show:

Well this little award was given to me last week not for anything I've particularly done, but for what has happened between 1966 when I made my first record and today. I've been working with these guys for the past four years and it's been a wonderful time, and I owe a good portion of this to the chaps behind me. I also owe a major portion of this to my good friend who has just joined me onstage... Jimmy Page.

On making Fate Of Nations:

Musically I'd become a bit technoed out. And I have a real desire to make things more emotive, to write songs from the heart again. I wanted to be the Robert Plant that sits up in the Welsh mountains and waits for Arthur.

I also went back to my old records and found Moby Grape and Buffalo Springfield still meaning something. I feel really good about this record. It reminds me of when I was young and musically naïve and emotionally open. And that's kind of where I'm at. This is a plot I want to keep now. As a retro Celt I'm sticking to this.

On performing Glastonbury in 1993:

We did the Bath Festival in Zeppelin a couple of times and this was very similar. The vibe was good and we had a perfect evening. I think the performance surprised a lot of people.

On David Coverdale:

I started looking at David Coverdale and realising I could do that. In fact that's what I do! That's me, I want my money back. And when I find him I shall get my money back! But you've got to laugh and say good old David. I thought he was Paul Rodgers, but he's not... he's me. Maybe next year he'll be Paul Rodgers.

On Page working with Coverdale:

This is my game and Jimmy's got his game. As long as he's happy I don't give a hoot who he's playing with. I think Page is re-instating himself as a very important guitarist. I wish the best for Jimmy and however he gets the best is entirely up to him.

I really want to see Jimmy do what he has to do to make him the ultimate guitarist again. Because he has been and still is the most fluent of rock guitarists. His construction of solos is superb and he's the king of riffs. Whatever it takes to be that then so be it because I love the old fool.

Difference between Robert and Jimmy in the early 90's:

Robert on Jimmy: With the Remasters – I get them but I don't play them all the way through. I do acknowledge the fact that they have improved, but I'm a bit sceptical as to whether or not it should be such a commercial adventure. And I do find Jimmy's constant sort of commenting about the lack of Led Zeppelin in the major sort of festival auditoriums in the country a bit boring. I really don't know the guy anymore. I guess that's the difference between myself and the whole Led Zeppelin myth as it is now. It is there in each of us. We should just continue in the best possible way to bring it out. I do it my way. Jimmy does it his.

Jimmy on Robert: Robert took a lot of swipes at me. When I came to the US to do publicity for the 'Outrider' album, all I got was 'Robert said this' and 'Robert said that'. I was there to talk about 'Outrider' and it was very tiresome. Somebody should tell Robert to keep his mouth shut.

Jimmy Page

On losing John Bonham:

There was a period after he died where I just didn't touch a guitar for ages. It just seemed to relate to everything that had happened. But then I called up my road manager one day and said 'Get the Les Paul out of storage'. He went to get it and the case was empty... It had been borrowed without permission and it eventually reappeared. But when he came back and said the guitar's missing, I thought that's it I'm finished. But thank God it turned up, and I began to pick up the pieces.

On making the soundtrack to Death Wish 2:

It was a real challenge trying to match music with visuals and very much a discipline. At one point I didn't think I'd be able to meet the deadline. I only had eight weeks to complete it. It really needs to be viewed as a soundtrack album and not as a solo album.

On forming a new band:

Obviously I want to get out and play. It may need some time to get together but I'm very keen to formulate something. It would be silly to even think of going on with Zeppelin without John. It would have been a total insult to John. I couldn't have played those numbers and looked around and seen someone else on the drums. It would not have been an honest thing to do.

On playing with Beck and Clapton on the ARMS tour:

There was such a great feeling on that tour. Personally I felt a lot of pressure because I didn't have a solo career like all the others. I just had a few tracks to work into the set.

But the fabulous thing was that it wasn't a competitive thing at all. The whole feeling of camaraderie and unity went right through to the road crews.

I did 'Stairway To Heaven' though there were no vocals. Nobody could sing it but Robert, it wouldn't be right. I did compose the music for it so I felt I could play it. Doing that was wonderfully emotional.

On playing with Roy Harper:

I felt pretty insecure after the group split and it was great to team up with someone like Roy. I guess that's why I played with him whenever I could. I knew him well and knew his stuff. When we did a production rehearsal at Brixton we went straight out and played acoustic at the Rock Garden. The Cambridge Folk Festival was another good one.

On forming The Firm:

Well I'd tried to get together with Paul earlier but he was doing a solo album. It really came together on the ARMS tour in America when we joined forces. We introduced 'Bird On A Wing' (later retitled 'Midnight Moonlight') which we then recorded for the first Firm album. We had various rehearsals for a drummer and bass player – even Rat Scabies came down for a jam. It started out as a one off project but we seem to be having fun with it.

On releasing Radioactive as a single and making a video:

We agreed to do a live performance video for 'Radioactive'. I know we never did singles in Zeppelin and people will say what a hypocrite. But the idea is to get seen and go out and play to people who have a lot of faith in me. Believe me there's been a lot of fans who have touched my heart. Especially on the ARMS tour. I realised the fans wanted me back.

On disbanding The Firm:

The initial idea was to prove we were still alive and kicking. So that aspect of it worked all right. But I don't think either of us wanted to get locked up into an album, tour, album set-up. Paul already had a solo career beforehand and I wanted to do other solo projects too.

On making Outrider:

It seemed a good time to do a solo record and use other players and vocalists. I'd actually planned 'Outrider' as a double set with more instrumentals. It was going to be one side rock n'roll, one side blues, one side acoustic and one side experimental. Some of the demos I was working on did actually go missing – they were stolen from my residence. It took quite a while to shape 'Outrider' and there was probably more work put into it than any album I've done in a long time.

On working with Jason Bonham:

He's improving all the time and learning his craft. I knew he'd be good. And there are definite similarities with his father. In fact during one rehearsal I turned round and called him John by mistake... I felt bad about it but he took it as a compliment.

On undertaking the Outrider tour:

The idea of the set is to make it into a chronological history of all the stuff I've been involved with – going as far back as The Yardbirds. In presenting the Zeppelin numbers I want to rearrange them a little to give them a little injection of new blood just to keep things interesting. The reaction to playing things like 'Stairway' has been just incredible.

On collaborating with David Coverdale:

After the Outrider project I wanted to do a really big album and get out on the road and show I was still around. So I'd been wading through scores of cassettes of singers and it was getting pretty daunting. I wasn't getting any inspiration at all, then someone from Geffen asked if I'd consider working with David. It seemed at least a good idea to get together and see how we got on.

Initially we just tried a few ideas and kept it behind closed doors. It was bound to cause preconceptions when two people like us get together. So we just kept it low key. Then we moved it all to Little Mountain Studios in Vancouver and brought in a rhythm section. That was the backbone to it all. The stuff came pouring out and we knew we had something that was good.

On the problems of instigating a Coverdale/ Page tour:

We've worked out a great set and I'm enjoying working on the Whitesnake songs and David is excellent. Right from the start if there was anything one of us felt uncomfortable about playing, we didn't try it. As for the cancellation of a US tour, it's the powers that be – the relative managements and others involved. All I know is what's recommended to me at the end of the day. I was up for playing anywhere but there's nothing on the table after our Japanese dates.

On using the new Tansperformance self tuning guitar:

The company had been trying to get hold of me for ages. They told me they had a guitar that tunes itself. I ignored them, but then they sent over a video and I said "Oh my God I've got one of those".

I could immediately see the possibilities in a multitude of situations. One was in writing a composition. It's nice to think about composing a song that's in more than one tuning. The other is live performance and not having to haul around several guitars for different tunings.

On sampling:

We were fair game for sampling. You could say we've been ripped off but I guess it's kept our music in the public's ear. And at least they sampled the best stuff.

John Paul Jones

On making Scream For Help:

Originally I thought I was going to write a proper film score and I thought I was going to do it electronically because I have my own studio. But then Michael Winner came up one day and said 'Right John, time to book the orchestra'. I said 'What orchestra?' and he said anything less than a 70 piece orchestra would make it sound like TV.

I had an idea for the first track 'Spaghetti Junction' and did a quick demo of it. I suddenly thought, what this needs is a guitar and then I thought, well there's only one guitarist so I rang up Pagey.

So while Jimmy was in the studio we also concocted another track 'Crackback' which is a bit of a throwback for us.

On the Atlantic 99 reunion:

In rehearsals it was quite incredible because I immediately struck up a rapport with Jason. It was funny how I slipped back into how I remembered it all. I went into a very old fill John and I used to do and Jason's right there with me. And it's one of those things that drummers and bassists do when they've been married ten years. But we went straight into it and we both looked around and shouted 'Chicago 1975!'. Because that's where it originated and Jason knew it so well.

On sampling of Zeppelin and copy bands:

I think they have all missed the point of diversity and experimentation that we had. That's what so dull about today's rock – it just doesn't look forward and explore new ideas. Originally we might have started out as a blues band but we took it from there. It was very much a team spirit. What made it interesting is that Led Zeppelin was the area between the four members.

On producing The Mission:

It was challenging to do it. They are a talented group that I felt I could influence. It was also fun getting up and jamming with them at the Astoria.

On projects in the 90's:

I recorded a Spanish outlet, a sort of an industrial flamenco band La Furu Del Baus. And something called Red Byrd. This is a group of early renaissance musicians. I'm well into experimental music. With computers. I've had commissions from the Electro Acoustic Music Association.

On playing with Manu Katche:

It must have been 10 years since I'd touched a bass in the studio. I'd simply reverted to it for Live Aid and the Atlantic reunion.

On being the quiet one:

That was brilliant for me. I cultivated it really, never looking the same for each tour. That way I could go anywhere I liked. Which is why I don't get mentioned too much in that absurd book (Hammer Of The Gods). I was never there!

Jonesy on the Remasters sets:

Well it all stands up doesn't it. As I've said before, Led Zeppelin was the common ground between four individual musicians. We all had different very wide ranging musical tastes. And the space between us – the area in the middle, was Led Zeppelin. And occasionally we were a bit loud, other times not. That was it really – it was the best bloody band there was!

Jonesy on working with Heart:

I did some work with Heart and got up and played with them. I picked up the bass for their version of 'What Is And What Should Never Be'. And when we did that, the whole place just went mad. It's not because I played that well, it just illustrates the Zeppelin myth. It's still a very potent thing. The songs, the legend, the name...

Jonesy on the MTV reunion:

To be honest I wasn't asked to do it. Nobody has rung me to tell me they are doing it. But good luck to them. Having read it in the papers was a bit odd. But it's not a Led Zeppelin reunion, it's a Jimmy Page and Robert Plant reunion... though I'm sure they'll be doing some Zeppelin material.

Robert on John Paul Jones:

I heard Jonesy got up with Lenny Kravitz at the MTV awards. Jonesy has a very dignified way of going about his career. He's quietly achieved a lot more than people can imagine. He's worked with R.E.M. and many independent bands and he's done a lot of stuff with contemporary bands in Spain. He just picks what he wants to do, which is great.

John Paul Jones with Lenny Kravitz

Other Asides To Merge In

Hammer Of The Gods:

Robert Plant: It's a mirror of someone else's frustrations. Richard Cole went around like the fifth or sixth member of the group causing havoc everywhere. It was reflected glory. A lot of things that were said happened after I was in bed. I was paranoid at losing my voice. But I was present at the mid shark incident. Me and my then wife walked past the door and saw Richard and the Vanilla Fudge with this girl.

Jimmy Page: I suppose I expected somebody would break ranks and betray the confidence but I didn't expect it to be Richard Cole. The thing that the remaining band members felt was that the whole humour of our life on the road had been portrayed as something really sordid. But it was nothing compared to his second book. That's a pack of lies and totally incorrect.

Kingdom Come:

Jimmy Page: Oh Kingdom Clone. I must admit there are a few moments when ghosts of myself can be heard.

Dread Zeppelin/ Kingdom Come:

Robert Plant: I don't think Dread Zeppelin can ever hope to scale the dizzy heights of mass media success. I think they're cute and very funny, but you can't take them seriously.

Kingdom Come were created by pompous videos with little Lenny the Dwarf looking as neat as possible, sounding like Led Zepp. But Dread Zeppelin... have you heard their version If Your Time Is Gonna Come? Incredible. Why we never did it that way I'll never know!

Stairway To Heaven:

Robert Plant: In Zeppelin we used to rehearse for about three days before a tour. Not a word would be said about that song. And then it would get to 6.30 on the day we were finishing and we were meant to be somewhere at 8pm, there'd be silence and then Jimmy would go 'Here we go then', and I'd say 'I'll be back in a sec' and nip to the toilet where I'd hear those jangling chords and go 'Aghh!'. It's a great song, written at the time for all the right reasons but try singing it ten years later and it's so sanctimonious. If you want to sing it for the next ten years you can – but I'm not.

We even played it as a reggae number in rehearsals – so you could say we did a Rolf Harris with it long before Rolf Harris!

Jimmy Page: I feel I owe it to myself to play it, and let the audience sing it, since Robert won't do it again. Funny guy Robert! But I'm proud to have written it and feel there's nothing wrong doing it this way.

Robert on Peter Grant:

Peter changed the rules. He rewrote the book. And he did so much for us that in 1975 he had to turn around and say 'Look guys there's nothing else I can do. We've had performing pigs, and high wire acts and all the wah, but there's nothing more I can do because you really now can go to Saturn'. We had twitchy times at the end, but I owe so much of my confidence to him because he pushed and cajoled all of us to make us what we were.

Led Zeppelin Remastered

The 1990 Remastering:

Jimmy Page: The idea was put to us by Atlantic and I was very keen to do it. Primarily because the CD's that had been issued were taken from poor tapes. It wasn't until I got into the studio and started work on them that I realised how into it I was. I worked wherever possible from the original master tapes. The essence of it all though is in the resequencing of the track listing, that whole 'same pictures with a different frame' ethic. Sitting there listening to it all was like reliving ten years of my life. Obviously a lot of memories came back. The track that seemed to really have an impact was 'Achilles Last Stand'. Everyone was going 'My God that really is brilliant'.

We never considered remixing them – the only remixing in any shape or form was for the 'Moby Dick'/'Bonzo's Montreux' creation. It was good to get some of those BBC tracks released, particularly 'Travelling Riverside Blues'. That seemed to resurface on the 'Outrider' tour.

The 1992 Remastering:

Jimmy Page: Straight after the completion of the Coverdale/Page album I took the time to remaster all the remaining tracks that we had missed doing in 1990. The reaction to the first set was incredible. It sold a million and a half copies and we got absolute rave reviews from the critics. That seemed quite weird after all these years. So the idea was to do a second set and then represent each album in remastered form individually. We approached the second set in the same way as the first. Engineer George Marino and I transferred the original analogue tapes to digital format, then we used some modern EQ's to make them sparkle. Then we pieced the tracks together so that the box has a certain flow – both aesthetically and technically.

There is one new track this time. 'Baby Come On Home' is an old blues number we'd tried on the first album sessions. The tape had been lost for years but mysteriously turned up. Robert's singing is excellent. He's just flying on it.

I did have that idea for a chronological live album after we lost John. It made sense but Robert didn't want it. So instead I compiled 'Coda'. I'd still like to do that live project but I won't spend hours and hours raking through tapes only for someone to say they don't want it released.

Final word on the release of the 10 CD's individually remastered in the 10 CD set The Complete Studio Recordings:

Of course I'm glad the music has stood the test of time. The 1970's was a very fortunate period to be in a creative band. It was an album's market which meant we could try anything. And we did.

Many people think of me just as a riff guitarist but I think of myself in broader terms. As a musician I think my greatest achievement has been to create unexpected melodies and harmonies within a rock n'roll framework. And as a producer I would like to be remembered as someone who was able to sustain a band of unquestionable individual talent and push it to the forefront during its working career. I think I really captured the best of our output, growth, change and maturity on tape.

The multifaceted gem that is Led Zeppelin.

Led Zeppelin Reunited

Reunions

Live Aid:

Robert Plant: Emotionally I was eating every word I uttered. And I was hoarse. I'd done three gigs on the trot before we got to Philadelphia. We rehearsed in the afternoon and by the time we got onstage my voice was well gone.

In a way it was just like it used to be. Apart from the fact that Bonzo wasn't there. When the curtains rolled back Jimmy still didn't have his guitar in his hand and I was wandering about thinking what my voice would sound like. So after 17 years and we still can't get it right!

In a way it was a wondrous thing, because it was a wing and a prayer gone wrong again. It was so much like a lot of Led Zeppelin gigs. But through it all, and through the rejection of ever having to do that song again, through all these compromises, I stood there smiling. I'd forgotten how much I'd missed it all. I'd be lying if I said I wasn't drunk on the whole thing. The fact that they were still chanting for us 15 minutes later and the fact that there were people crying all over the place... it was something far more powerful than words can convey

Jimmy Page: It did feel like one hour's rehearsal after seven years, but to be part of Live Aid was wonderful. I think it was great that we did it. Our spirit was there as much as everybody else's.

Atlantic Reunion:

Jimmy Page: As far as the rehearsals went it was fabulous. The trouble was we were due to go on at a certain time and that got delayed by nearly two hours. By then I was suffering from bad stage fright. You find yourself biting your fingernails, telling people to leave you alone. Another tragedy of the night was the TV sound which completely lost the keyboards. I found that unforgivable. Aside from the fact that it was a great thrill for Jason.

I found the whole thing very disappointing. A huge amount of reasoning for doing the Atlantic show was to make up for the shortcomings of Live Aid, and at the end of the day we still couldn't win. It's a shame because those rehearsals beforehand in New York showed just how good we could still be.

Atlantic 88:

Robert Plant: The night before at the rehearsal it had been spectacular. What happened on the night? I can't tell you. I have no idea. I'm sitting in exactly the same spot as you asking the great void Why? But a lot of people thought they saw something great.

Jason Bonham: It was just the most amazing night for me. And I make no bones about it. If Zepp re-form tomorrow and I get the call I'd be off. I'd be a fool not to really, don't you think?

Robert Plant on reuniting with Page and Jones for his daughter's 21st birthday party:

When I got up with those two at Carmen's birthday party, Page's playing was so good. I had a big lump in my throat. I had forgotten how he tears into things. When he plays in those circumstances it's unbelievable. He's had these fluctuating times when his nerves have been so bad he couldn't play. But that night we were so good. It gave me something I hadn't had for a long time.

Peter Grant on the reunions:

As far as the Live Aid and Atlantic reunions were concerned – I watched them both and thought they were very sad. Dreadful. The latter show was particularly horrendous. I know for a fact that right up to until five minutes before the band were due to go onstage, Robert was refusing to sing 'Stairway To Heaven'. And he was totally out of order on that. Atlantic invited me to attend but I declined.

Peter Grant on the aftermath of the split:

Well the band was no longer there and I couldn't manage three different people. I started doing a few things with Robert – I made the solo deal for him in 81/82. But I could not go on and to be honest I wasn't in any shape health wise. Much of the 80's was a period of blackness for me. I feel fitter now than I have in a while and I'm collaborating with Malcolm McClaren on a film project that will be based on my life in rock management.

Robert Plant on regrouping for rehearsals in Bath 1986:

We did try and get together for a week in Bath early in 1986. But as much as he wanted to do it, it wasn't the right time for Pagey to do it. He had just finished the second Firm album and I think he was a bit confused. What we did sounded a bit like David Byrne. I played bass on it. But the whole thing dematerialised. Jimmy had to change the battery on his wah-wah every

two and a half songs. And then the drummer Tony Thompson got injured in a car accident. It just wasn't to be. For it to have worked in Bath I'd have had to have been far more patient than I had been for years.

The reunion after the Remasters project:

Jimmy Page: When the 4 CD box set came out we all had a year off. Robert put his band on hold until the future. I had nothing in the pipeline, and Jonesy was keen to do it. Robert's manager thought he was going to do it. We had a meeting in Robert's manager's office and for some reason he wasn't keen on Jason. Jonesy was. I suggested Simon Phillips though I'd have preferred Jason. Robert nominated a drummer and we thought, well great at least he's considering it. So Jonesy and I left the meeting to get a video of this drummer so we could compare notes. But by the following day Robert had changed his mind.

If it wasn't going to happen then when it was wide open for us to do it, then I can't see it ever happening. It seemed a logical step except for Robert who felt it was going to harm his solo career. That's his decision, so that's it.

Robert Plant on reuniting with Jimmy:

I often think I'd like to rehearse with Jimmy until it was really good and then do one quick blast through. But it would have to be incredibly good music. And that's what I'd need to be able to go out and call it Page and Plant. That's how it would have to be, the real new Zeppelin. And the possibility of that is years away... if at all.

Jimmy Page on reuniting with Robert:

I've always been very proud of the music. I don't think you can have such a rewarding experience as a musician than to actually

have been in a band like that, and to make music which has stood up to the test of time. I love the music and it's always going to be a part of me. It was such a major part of my life. So I'd be prepared to do it, who knows?

I'm sure there's a lot of people who would like to see us together again. Me being one of them. I've never doubted for a minute that if Robert and I sat down and started writing that we could come up with some good stuff.

The MTV filming: working with an Egyptian ensemble:

Jimmy Page: I was getting shivers listening to the Egyptians playing. Just the whole texture that was going on. We know what we can achieve now and there is so much more we can do.

Robert Plant: During Kashmir in the film there's a close up of the solo violin player, and that man's face – he was so far gone. He was so proud and it's great to work with musicians who are so proud of their roots and they're not normally in a position to extend it into this area. They have been fantastic.

The MTV reunion

Jimmy Page: I'd been wanting to work with Robert again for a long time. It was a long time coming. 14 years really! And now the time is right. But we both agreed that if we were going to do something then it had to be new, and that if we were to look at the old material then we'd have to treat it as an old picture ready for a new frame.

Robert Plant: We said 'Hey let's try this and let's just see how it goes'. And we found that the communion was a little more fluent now – even more than it was way back when. We found that we arrived at decisions very quickly, without much pussyfooting around... but there was never any question of us just rolling out the barrel. It had to be new.